The Roundtable Pulpit

---

*Where Leadership
and Preaching Meet*

John S. McClure

*Abingdon Press
Nashville*

THE ROUNDTABLE PULPIT
WHERE LEADERSHIP AND PREACHING MEET

Copyright © 1995 by Abingdon Press

This book is printed on recycled, acid-free paper.

Library of Congress Cataloging-in-Publication Data

McClure, John S., 1952–
    The roundtable pulpit: where leadership and preaching meet / John S. McClure.
        p.   cm.
    Includes bibliographical references and index.
    ISBN 0-687-01142-6 (alk. paper)   2/96
    1. Collaborative preaching.   I. Title.
BV4235.C64M33   1995
251—dc20   95-3956
                                                                              CIP

95 96 97 98 99 00 01 02 03 04 05—10 9 8 7 6 5 4 3 2 1

MANUFACTURED IN THE UNITED STATES OF AMERICA

In loving memory of my mother,
Margaret Messer McClure,
who loved words and the Word.

CONTENTS

PREFACE

Collaborative preaching is a method that involves members of a congregation in sermon brainstorming. Preaching becomes a "rhetoric of listening"[1] through which the biblical interpretations and theological insights of the congregation find a voice in the pulpit. When used over a period of time, collaborative preaching empowers members of a congregation to claim as their own the ideas, forms of religious experience, and theological vision articulated from the pulpit. Preaching, therefore, becomes a focal point for congregational self-leadership and mission.

Browne Barr was the first writer to advocate a collaborative approach to preaching, at the 1963 Lyman Beecher lectures entitled *Parish Back Talk*. He advocated a "sermon seminar" to assist the preacher in sermon preparation.[2] Later, in *The Ministering Congregation*, he and co-pastor Mary Eakin described how the sermon seminar could become an integral part of an entire progam of lay ministry.[3] Homiletician John Killinger advised that collaborative sermon preparation is a way to recover congregational interest in preaching.[4] Collaborative models were also suggested by theoreticians of parish dialogue such as Reuel Howe and Clyde Reid.[5]

More recently, Don Wardlaw identified collaboration as a way to help the preacher correlate today's social context with the ancient social context of biblical passages.[6] Pamela Ann Moeller, in her book entitled *A Kinesthetic Homiletic: Embodying Gospel in Preaching,* includes corporate sermon preparation as an integral part of her performative homiletic.[7]

My approach goes further by investigating the implications of collaborative preaching for congregational leadership and homiletical method. In chapter 1 my goal is to identify ways that preaching can empower congregations. I develop a brief public theology of preaching and highlight certain aspects of the theology of the Word that are suggested by a collaborative approach to sermon preparation. In chapter 2 I analyze aspects of homiletical theory and provide reasons for taking sermon preparation out of the pastoral study and into the context of roundtable conversation.

In the final four chapters I set forth a collaborative homiletical method. Chapter 3 uses the image of the roundtable to shape a general theory of collaborative preaching. Chapter 4 describes a collaborative process of sermon brainstorming (the sermon roundtable) that can be used in any congregation. Chapter 5 provides examples of the kinds of conversational pulpit language that model collaborative preaching in practice. Chapter 6 is a case study that illustrates how to make use of the conversation that takes place in a brainstorming group in the preparation of an actual sermon.

The reader who is interested only in the practical aspects of this homiletical method can skip to chapter 4. In order to correctly understand this method of preaching, however, it is helpful to read the theology and theory that is set forth in the first three chapters.

I will not suggest that preachers actually hold conversations from the pulpit or that they attempt two or three party "dialogue sermons." My goal is simply to move closer to a model of single-party preaching that includes the actual language and dynamics of collaborative conversation on biblical texts, theology, and life.

I assume that the Bible is at the center of the preaching process. I do not advocate a topical approach to preaching that might be the result of measuring the actual implied needs and wants in segments of a congregation. Neither, however, do I encourage a narrowly expository approach in which the Bible is treated as a kind of "husk" within which are timeless exegetical "kernels" that are the Word of God. The good news of the gospel emerges in the theological event of interpretation, not in the critical practice of exegesis (though, of course, these are not mutually exclusive). That is why I place such a high premium on the conversation between the biblical text, theology, and life of real people.

It is my experience that collaborative preaching increases the authority of the Bible in a congregation at the same time that it provides an excellent opportunity for basic Bible education. Toward these ends preachers and sermon brainstorming groups can make good use of the lectionary in sermon planning and preparation. The discipline of the lectionary ensures that the entire biblical canon will be covered in collaborative preaching.

This book begins somewhere in the middle of my own reflection on the problems of pastoral leadership in relation to preaching. I do not take the time to describe in this book the various contexts of ministry from which these problems arise. The reader is spared a litany of congregational case studies and a recounting of the many conversations that I have had with clergy and laity on this subject. Instead, the book begins at the point where I am searching for biblical and theological language that will help to describe and interpret an emerging practical theological hypothesis: that the best way to empower congregations for ministry and mission is through the use of collaborative forms of leadership and preaching.

I am very grateful to many colleagues and friends for the trajectories of thought that make their way into this book. Barbara Tesorero and Virgil Cruz prompted me to involve laity in a team-taught course several years ago. This course first introduced me to the value of collaboration in sermon preparation. I am indebted to Johanna (van Wijk) Bos for conversations on the idea of "hospitality to the stranger" in the Old Testament, and for her bibliography on this subject. Thanks to Joan Jacobs, Burton Cooper, David Hester, Amy Plantinga Pauw, Barbara McDonald, Tim Staveteig, and Paul Franklyn for their fine editorial counsel on various drafts of the manuscript. I am also grateful to many friends in the parish who have tried this approach to preaching in its various permutations and provided me with suggestions. Special thanks to members of the 1994 Homiletical Feast in Dallas, Texas, who helped me to refine several of my categories and procedures and to Bill Harris, who drew my attention to the similarities between this approach to preaching and current brainstorming methods used in various corporations.

Although I set forth something in this book to which I am deeply committed, it is meant to be an open model. It is conceivable, even probable, that there are many ways to be truly collaborative in leadership and preaching, and that my convictions only represent one approach, or a partial approach. As I note in chapter 5, "repair" is one of the fundamental dynamics of any roundtable conversation, and I welcome the additions or corrections of those who have had different experiences and who represent different traditions.

Preaching and Empowerment

I would be disappointed if this book provides only an innovative technique or model of preaching. I want to help the preacher come to an understanding of the nature of biblical proclamation that can become the centerpiece of an effective form of congregational leadership and, perhaps, a repaired form of Christian community.

Many challenges face preachers in North American churches today. "Mainstream" preachers have discovered that their denominations are disenfranchised within the American religious landscape.[1] Whether mainstream or not, preachers are confronted daily with pressing environmental, social and psychological issues. Everywhere, there is renewed interest in preaching that displays urgent prophetic, evangelical, and pastoral commitments.

In response to this situation, biblical scholars and homileticians stress the need for more exacting and challenging messages from the pulpit. Walter Brueggemann, in *The Prophetic Imagination,* urges prophetic preachers to summon congregations to become alternative communities within the dominant culture.[2] William Sloane Coffin, in *A Passion for the Possible: A Message to the U. S. Churches,* pleads with preachers to become theologically inspired activists who take clear stands on today's pressing social and political issues.[3] William Willimon, in *Peculiar Speech: Preaching to the Baptized,* encourages preachers to help congregations articulate their ecclesial identity and confront American society as an evangelistic and missionary counterculture.[4] J. Randall Nichols, in *The Restoring Word: Preaching as Pastoral Communication,* advises pastoral preachers to lead congregations "to take responsibility both for themselves and for the piece of the world that is given into their care."[5] We should not assume, however, that these strong commitments require that preachers become lone voices shouting in a wilderness. In each instance, our task should become more community-centered, so that we empower others when proclaiming the gospel. I am reminded that these community-based concerns are echoed in the writing of those who have lived and worked in base Christian communities in Central America.[6]

According to leadership theorists, different situations require different forms of leadership.[7] Autocratic leadership, for instance, is effective in emergency situations (the health or welfare of a member is threatened, the furnace needs immediate repair) or instructional situations (the lay liturgists need to know the church's polity on ordination procedures). Autocratic leadership is also effective in situations where the imposition of a personal vision is accepted by followers as an avenue to excellence (a choir preparing for a major choral work, a church theatrical production).

Consultative and collaborative forms of leadership, however, are more effective when leaders hope to build the kind of strategic prophetic, evangelistic, and pastoral commitments that are needed in our churches today. Situational studies of leadership demonstrate that collaborative forms of leadership are particularly effective in building lay commitment and lay leadership. Collaborative leadership is also helpful in situations where decisions involve personal or institutional risk. If we desire our congregations to claim countercultural identities, risk evangelical or social action, or commit to fundamental organizational changes, we must become collaborative in every dimension of our leadership, including preaching.

Collaborative leadership is empowering leadership. According to Rollo May, empowerment includes two aspects: integrative power (power with others), and nutritive power (power for others).[8] *Integrative* power includes all the ways that leaders form alliances of power that will benefit members of the community. It is the way a leader connects the narrow concerns within the community with other communities and with the public interest at large. *Nutritive* power includes all the ways that leaders invite or permit others to assume responsibility for the direction of their own lives and to assume leadership roles themselves. It is the way a leader includes followers in an active role as interpreters of their situation and as decision-makers about their own future.

Integrative Power

When your preaching empowers a congregation it must express power *with* others. It must invite church members to stand with others who live in very different situations, and help church members to find others who stand with them in their situation. In other words, preaching must reach across boundaries and connect people, creating new communities of commitment and hope.[9]

A Public Theology of Preaching

Public theologians assert that the central task of the church's ministry is to "resist the gravitational pull of privatization"[10] and to re-connect the gospel message with the public realm. According to Parker Palmer, the word *public* is a metaphor for the "ebb and flow of the company of strangers, which happens in relatively unstructured and disorderly ways: on the city streets, in parks and squares, at festivals and rallies, and shopping malls, neighborhoods and voluntary associations."[11] Public life is a "messy 'middle layer' " between formal social or political institutions and the private realm "from which the stranger qua stranger is excluded."[12] According to Palmer, we cannot be spiritually alive unless we venture forth into the public realm and encounter the strangers who live there.[13]

Patrick R. Keifert, in his book *Welcoming the Stranger: A Public Theology of Worship and Evangelism,* identifies three ways to think of strangers in relation to the church: (1) as the outsiders who come from beyond the church itself, (2) as "inside strangers" who "remain outside the intimate group that usually makes up most of the leadership in a congregation," and (3) as a description of "the irreducible difference between two persons that exists in any encounter."[14] The stranger is the *other* who presents us with what Edward Farley calls the "mysterious presence of something which contests my projecting meanings on it, an unforeseeable depth which . . . cannot be cognitively or emotionally mastered."[15]

Theologically, the stranger represents both the Holy Other and the human *other:* the dual foci of the great commandment. As Christians, we are commanded to love God, the Holy Other, who is the ground of all love and justice. We are also commanded to love neighbor, the human other whose vulnerability invites us beyond ourselves into the realm of compassion, suffering, and responsibility.[16]

Practically speaking, who are some of these human strangers? They are all around us, inside and outside the church. There's Martha who, at age 68, with no children, battles loneliness. There's Carl who sleeps some nights at the homeless shelter and has trouble with demons. There's Mary, a lesbian, who wonders what to do with her sexuality in both culture and church. There's Bill, a busy lawyer who is often angry and suffers under the oppressive weight of the upper middle-class rat race. There's Clara, a heavy smoker dying from lung cancer, living in fear and denial because her family owns part of a huge tobacco interest. There's Bob, a missionary who sometimes wonders if what he does really makes a difference. There's Jenny, a twelve-year-old, who feels a great love for God and who wants to give more to the church and to the poor. There's Carol, a single parent of three children, struggling at the bottom of the pay scale. And there are many, many others sitting in the pews next to us and living in the world beyond the sanctuary doors.

To ask these people what kinds of interpretive spins they put on the gospel of Jesus Christ is to embark on a homiletical adventure in the public realm. If we ask what in particular they see in the gospel that is meaningful for their lives, we will hear all kinds of things, some of which will seem to us to be heretical. Yet if we as preachers dare to involve these diverse folk in a roundtable process through which they begin to come to terms with the gospel and with each other, we will create an opportunity for a preachable Word to emerge that may bind the church and the world together in solidarity and hope. This is the adventure that follows when we take the discernment of the Word into the public arena where strangers within and beyond the church hold us accountable to the unique reality and particularity of their own spiritual experience.

There are at least two primary ways to miss out on this adventure in the public realm. One way is to "try to gain enough power to enforce our own standards on the alien experience."[17] According to Palmer, "(this) takes the form of . . . controlling the definition of 'orthodoxy' and suppressing all signs of 'heresy' . . . ."[18] Homiletically, it takes the form of sermons that rehearse timeless exegetical pearls of wisdom and dated doctrine, or that repeat platitudes and formulas that are supposed to have magical efficacy.

The second way to miss encountering the stranger in our midst is to create and fortify something called a "private life."[19] Palmer asserts that "instead of encountering, engaging, and growing from the diversity within and outside us . . ." we can try "to avoid it altogether by building high walls of privatism."[20]

More often than not the church mirrors our society by becoming an extension of the private realm, a haven of orthodoxy or an extended family that provides a comfortable escape from the public realm. Congregational life is given over to what Richard Sennett calls the "ideology of intimacy,"[21] the idea that "the purpose of human life is the fullest development of one's individual personality, which can take place only within . . . intimate relationships."[22]

When this is the case, worship and preaching tend to go in one of two different directions. The first direction is toward anonymity and bureaucratization. Worship becomes an aesthetic or entertainment experience in which one is left alone in one's private world and is engaged by a constant barrage of entertaining or aesthetic stimuli. Sermons resemble after-dinner speeches or become moments of highly crafted oratorical or artistic wonder.

At the other end of the continuum, worship and preaching become attempts to *recreate* the private sphere in what Mark Searle calls "the pseudo-family atmosphere cultivated by suburban fellowshipping, or in the more intensive emotional atmosphere of renewal groups."[23] According to Searle such worship services are often "smoothly orchestrated celebrations of suburbia" with choirs, folk groups and "easy listening" music, firm handshakes and abundant lay ministers, or more radical folk and rock and roll formats.[24] Worship becomes what Robert Bellah calls a "life-style enclave."[25] Preaching is usually folksy and intimate in style, with an abundance of storytelling and heartrending self-disclosure by the preacher.

Throughout such worship and preaching, God is usually domesticated. To use Palmer's language:

God is made an inmate of the private realm. Gone is the strangeness of God, the wild and alien quality of holiness that was so well known to primal peoples (witness the Hebrew

Bible). In its place is an image of God as a member of the church family circle. God is like a kind and comfortable old friend, a God who comforts and consoles us—and even reinforces our prejudices—but in no way challenges or stretches our lives.[26]

Unwittingly, many churches create a private realm in which neither the stranger nor the strangeness of God has any place, a den of comfort in which parishioners can remain anonymous and not have to encounter anything that is strange or alien.

Keifert points out how the stranger was very important to the worship and preaching of Israel.[27] Worship was not a human device to hold God at bay, but a gift from God of God's unfathomable self. This gift was offered in both the preaching and the worship of the people of God and was available to all those whom God invited. The stranger was always invited to worship, and the needs and hopes of the stranger filled the prophetic proclamation that guided the people of God in their journey away from sectarianism and nationalism toward becoming a truly universal religion.

Recent attempts to develop public theologies suggest several commitments that we as preachers must have if we are to form deeper alliances of spiritual power between the community of faith and the world in which we live. First, we must attempt in our preaching to reconnect the private realm and the public realm. We must strive to take ourselves and those around us who have become satisfied with living cloistered lives of religious and personal self-protection, into a teaching-learning encounter with the strangers within the church and just beyond the walls of the church building. We must seek out the unique, strange and sometimes bizarre interpretations of the gospel that are around us in our culture, in the minds and hearts of good church people, and latent within the recesses of our own lives, and come to terms with these in the pulpit. We do not do this in order to appear contemporary and inclusive or to make preaching seem more relevant. We do it because we believe that the Word of God becomes known when real people (who are in reality more different than they are alike), strive to discern and express their solidarity in Christ. We do this in order to cultivate within the theological imagination of our Christian communities an understanding of the *other*, the stranger, as the potential bearer of wisdom and insight, rather than the bearer of values that are threatening.

Second, we must cultivate a sense in our worship and preaching that our proclamation of the redemptive work of Christ is in continuity with the creative Word of God, the Word that created and breathed life into the world.[28] Preachers must never proclaim Christ as if Christ's redemptive work related only to a selective history of salvation. Our homiletical imaginations must become large enough to embrace the relatively chaotic depths of both the inner life and the public life. In order to accomplish this, the focus of preaching must move from the center of the Christian community to its margins, from the pastor's study to the sanctuary door. The preacher must stand at the boundary of the community, at the place where its cultural-linguistic mythos is being engaged and challenged by the often-silenced voices of strangers and of the "God beyond the gods." Such preaching struggles to discern what the redemptive power of the Christian story is in *this* world and in *this* history.

Third, we must allow the Word of God in preaching to critique many aspects of the culture of privatism in which we live. We must be careful, however, not to create a boundary that marks the church off from the *world* and its *history*. Our baptism does not isolate us as a sectarian cult that shares no common humanity with other people. The ashes on our forehead at Ash Wednesday should remind us of this.

We can, however, celebrate the theological and ethical distinctiveness of the Christian community as a truly public, universal, and non-sectarian community, and work against all attempts to domesticate both God and Christian religious experience. The God whom we preach does not tolerate any attempt within the culture or the church to privatize the gospel message. We proclaim that there is a clear difference between public faith and privatized religion.

In order to overcome the weight of privatization we must demonstrate continuously the deep, transformative *relationship* between the historic symbols of the Christian faith and the realities of our public life. This is the only kind of catechesis that is appropriate to a truly monotheistic and universal religion. Preachers must show how Christian symbols reach out and encompass not only the community of the baptized, but also all of those who breathe the same air that we breathe.

Finally, we must preach in such a way that the church becomes a community of both ecclesial and public memory. Not only should our preaching remember and celebrate the history of the church, and the history of a particular congregation, but we must also remember especially the things that the culture and church of privatism tend to forget.[29] Christine Smith, in her book *Preaching as Weeping, Confession and Resistance,*[30] encourages the preacher to remember the radical equality of all human beings before God. She invites preachers to remember the disabled, the sick, the aged, the dying, the homosexual, the abused, the unsuccessful, and all who have been relegated to the margins of our society. In like manner Elaine Ramshaw, in her book *Ritual and Pastoral Care,* encourages forms of worship that express a "critical memory." Instead of recalling the history of the conquerors, preachers and liturgists must remember those who have suffered unjustly on behalf of righteousness and truth, both within and beyond the church.[31]

Nutritive Power

The pathway to integrative power runs through nutritive power. Preachers must not stand on platforms and harangue congregations for being victims of privatization. Instead, we must slowly pry open the private realm by placing people face to face with one another in a context in which otherness, rather than homogeneity, is valued and taken seriously. We must help to recreate the church as a learning community where Christians share power and permit themselves to be instructed by one another's differences.

The only way to accomplish this is to include others in the biblical-theological interpretation of their situation and in the making of decisions about their own future. This requires that we take a good hard look at *how* we prepare and preach sermons and how we lead our congregations. *We must look at the relationship between our preaching and our leadership.*

Leadership and preaching work together in at least three important ways: (1) to embody the kind of *relationships* that are to exist in the community, (2) to indicate the *roles* that members of the community can expect to play in decision-making and planning, and (3) to demonstrate the form of *persuasion* that is central to bringing about change in the community. In order to express nutritive empowerment, or power *for* others, both leadership and preaching must embody *face-to-face relationships, participative roles* in decision-making, and *interactive forms of persuasion.*

1. Face-to-face Relationships

Many congregations are marked by a relative absence of face-to-face relationships between leaders and followers, preachers and hearers. In the case of the congregation a culture of anonymity develops, and *alienated* forms of clergy-laity relationship usually prevail. Alienation is a mark of "leadership at a distance"[32] and "task leadership."[33] Such leadership is formal, impersonal, and instrumental, centering on task accomplishment and conformity to policies and rules. Leaders usually settle for hierarchical patterns of relationship that require a minimum of personal interaction. Preachers become lone prophets of a divinely inspired Word and expect obedience, or at least compliance, once this Word has been spoken.

At the other extreme, leader-follower and preacher-hearer relationships can become *symbiotic*. When this happens, leaders and preachers tend to assume that everyone in their congregations are extensions of their personalities. The church and its mission are identified solely with the personality of the leader. Preaching feeds the "cult of personality." Preachers globalize their own experience and identify the hearer's personality with their own.[34]

There is, however, another option. Leader and follower, preacher and hearer, can work to establish face-to-face relationships as a response to the vision of righteousness that prevails in Christian *koinonia* (partnership). Face-to-face relationships are rooted in a profound respect of the other person as truly *other* rather than as an instrumental object or a self-projection. In face-to-face relationships, preachers and hearers do not relate to one another in order to achieve obedience or identification. Rather, they strive to "come to terms" with one another.

2. Participative Roles

Nutritive power is shared power. This means that all members of a community, from the center to the margins, must be allowed to participate in the interpretation of the community's mission and in decision-making.[35] In order for this to occur, preachers must give the congregation a role in the *discernment* of the Word to be preached. This means that preachers must revise their traditional understanding of the Word of God in preaching in several crucial ways.

A COMMUNAL WORD

Several biblical and historical precedents convey the idea that the Word of God should be discerned by the community rather than by individuals. It was principally the *community,* and not the *individual,* who became the curator of the Word during the time of the Babylonian exile. Hebrew prophecy was transformed from "direct inspired utterance" to communal interpretation.[36] According to Stanley Hauerwas:

> Prophecy is no longer relegated to individuals, but now becomes a task of the whole community as the community seeks to discern and interpret events in the light of God's past relation with them . . . . For such a community, prophecy is no longer solely the role of specific individuals, although individual prophets will, I hope, still be present. It is the community itself that is now prophetic.[37]

This radical assumption, that *all members of the community have an interpretive and proclamatory vocation,* was reasserted during the Reformation in the concept of the priesthood of all believers. Members of the community of faith should not rely passively on the wisdom of either itinerant or commissioned preachers.

Typically, contemporary preachers act under the explicit or tacit assumption that they are commissioned as professional interpreters and proclaimers. Their task is to sit down alone, with books by other professionals, or sometimes in a lectionary study group of fellow professionals, and prayerfully read and study the Bible with sermon preparation in mind. They do this in order to discern a Word that can be delivered faithfully in the midst of the community on Sunday morning.

If we take seriously the potential interpretative and proclamatory vocation of all members of the congregation, however, then the preached Word cannot be properly divined from the center of the community by a member of a guild of professional preachers. We must actually allow members of the congregation to participate in the discernment of the preached Word. Otherwise, what is repeated over and over again from the pulpit is an interpretation of the biblical story that is the private property of the preacher and an elite corps of biblical interpreters.

If the church is to claim its own identity as a community of the Word, preachers must engage in the kind of actual, critical collaboration that brings the reality of the community's life to bear in biblical interpretation. Collaboration is not the same as consultation. It is not using the insights of others to shore up the preacher's homiletical messages. Collaboration means that others may, indeed, have something to teach the preacher, since there is no way that the preacher can sit where they sit. Another person's reading of the gospel may transform the preacher's interpretation entirely. When preachers have interacted with these interpretations, they may find themselves in the pulpit on Sunday morning proclaiming a very different Word than they otherwise could have expected.

The Word of God, therefore, is a communal Word when it is discerned, not from the center of the community by professional preachers, but from the margins of the community by a collaboration of everyday preachers who are developing as maturing Christian disciples. This Word can then be proclaimed from the center of the community by a preacher whose primary goal is to influence these everyday preachers toward more and more interpretative and proclamatory faithfulness.

AN EMERGENT WORD

Because the Word of God is communal it emerges in the process of dialogue that takes place within the community. The Word is brought forth in the give-and-take of conversations in which the meaning and purpose of the gospel is being sought. This Word is not an individual *mandate* or *insight*. Rather, it emerges as what philosopher Emmanuel Levinas calls a "coming to terms"[38] that occurs in the course of conversations by the proclamatory community that are focused on discerning the Word of God for the community. To say that the Word of God is a "coming to terms" does not necessarily mean that it is a consensus. Coming to terms is a quality of *relationships* more than it is a quality of ideas. It implies that members of the community of the Word decide on ways to stand *with* and stand *for* one another by claiming tentative *directions* of thought and action as God's Word.

To say that the Word of God is emergent is also to say that it is always changing, as the community interprets scripture, tradition, theology, and life. New Testament scholar Peter Stuhlmacher has often emphasized that "the gospel is always before us."[39] We can never completely come to terms with the gospel message. The gospel of Jesus Christ presents us with new possibilities for meaning, life, and mission each day as the community changes, expands, and includes more diversity in its interpretive procedures.

A "REAL" WORD

As I have suggested, members of a congregation bring very different, strange, and sometimes bizarre interpretations of the Word of God into church every Sunday. Though they can consume enormous amounts of energy, these interpretations must find their way into the proclamation of the preacher. Since the diverse particularity of experience is what constitutes the fabric of reality itself, the exclusion of these interpretations of the gospel from preaching means that the Word of God in preaching *loses its reality*. It may become a lot of "sound and fury" that signifies very little of anything to anybody.

Collaborative proclamation is designed to bring *more reality* into the pulpit on Sunday morning. The Word of God is an enfleshed, incarnate Word, not an abstract or esoteric Word. Sermons speak directly about what is happening in the congregation: struggles to understand the meaning of the gospel, emerging commitments in light of this struggle, and forms of faithful practice that are being considered or have already begun. In collaborative preaching the particular fears, anxieties, hopes, celebrations, quirks, longings, needs, insights, hopes, and sufferings that are present in the congregation and in the world are "looked in the face."[40] When this happens, the Word of God becomes a *real* Word, spoken in the closest possible relation to the actual life situation of both the congregation and individuals.

3. Interactive Persuasion

Leadership and preaching are *persuasive*.[41] Persuasion is rhetorical activity designed to effect a change of attitude and to motivate new forms of action. Persuasion becomes *coercion* when the hearer's freedom of choice is destroyed through fear, peer pressure, or double binding.[42] Persuasion becomes *manipulation* when the hearer's choice is seduced through subconscious ploys, idealized associations with the rich or famous (or the persuader), faulty promises, or contrived situations of perceived choice. Persuasive communication, therefore, walks a tightrope between coercion and manipulation.

In face-to-face relationships, persuasive leaders learn to respect the spiritual freedom and power of the *other* in the communication process. They learn that persuasion is a two-way street and that followers may persuade leaders as well. Persuasion is not an action *on* someone, but an action *with* someone.

Later we will experience the *interactive* language of roundtable conversation as a form of persuasion that can empower rather than coerce or manipulate the hearer. When it grows out of an interactive process of sermon brainstorming, this language provides a dialogical rhetoric that can be used in single-party preaching.

The Preacher as Host

The charismatic image of the preacher as prophet is easily misunderstood in our generation. The kind of authority that issues from charisma has been negatively associated in our day with authoritarian leaders such as Hitler or various cult leaders. Charismatic leadership in the New Testament churches, however, was neither authoritarian nor sectarian in nature. In fact, it seems that precisely the opposite was the case. In many instances the charismatic leadership of both Jesus and Paul undercut the false authority of those who represented authoritarian forms of leadership or the narrow-mindedness of sectarianism. Jesus and Paul disputed the authority of those who failed to demonstrate the fundamental quality of Christian leadership established in Matthew 20:26-27: "Whoever wishes to be great among you must be your servant, and whoever wishes to be first among you must be your slave." Hans von Campenhausen, in his seminal study of Pauline authority entitled *Ecclesiastical Authority and Spiritual Power in the Early Church* paints a compelling "picture of a form of charismatic egalitarianism that existed in the early church in which episcopal hierarchy was spurned in favor of charismatic servant leaders."[43]

By the time of the Ephesian letter, *charisma* had been democratized into various forms of spiritual gifts (*charis*, Eph. 4:7). To the charismatic apostles and prophets were added evangelists and pastors-and-teachers (Eph. 4:11). Within the household of faith, therefore, a broad range of activities began to receive the indirect undergirding of servant-charisma.

Charismatic individuals in all ages, however, often have made iconoclastic and revelatory claims to authority that tend to move toward closure and finality in matters of truth.[44] Because claims to having transcendental truth carry the seeds of idolatry and authoritarianism, charismatic individuals in the early church were managed within the framework of another kind of authority and leadership. This form of authority was rooted deeply in the biblical tradition, and gave expression to the dynamic, open, and universal nature of biblical faith as a monotheistic religion. This was the authority of the leader as *host* within the religious community.

Michael White, in an important study of social authority in the early church, shows how charismatic apostles such as Paul and Peter showed deference to the traditional authority of the host within the family household.[45] Because the earliest Christian congregations met in homes, authority was vested in familial activities of hospitality. White shows how the social conventions of hospitality and patronage were well developed in the early church and included "receiving . . . preaching, mutual exhortation, and communal fellowship around the dinner table which also served as the center of eucharistic anamnesis," and "sending on one's way."[46] In Philippians (1:5; 4:15) Paul calls such actions of hospitality "partnership" *(koinonia)* in the gospel. Elsewhere they are called acts of service *(diakonia)* and expressions of love *(agape)* (Rom. 16:1-2; Philem. 4-6).

In addition to the house churches which served primarily upper- or middle-class Christians, there were also "tenement churches" which "consisted entirely of the urban underclass, primarily slaves and former slaves."[47] Hosting in these churches appears to have been shared among several co-hosts.[48]

The itinerant, charismatic prophet, therefore, was always "hosted." Often, the host was an itinerant prophet who had taken up residence. The host, therefore, understood the nature of charismatic authority and was able to keep charismatic individuals from within and beyond the community from claiming premature closure with respect to Christian truth. The host accomplished this by placing the revelations of the charismatic individual into dialogue with members of the community who had very different spiritual gifts *(charis),* and by constantly welcoming into conversation others within and beyond the community who claimed to have insights into the nature of the Christian message.

John Koenig, in his book *New Testament Hospitality: Partnership with Strangers as Promise and Mission,* asserts that the entire sweep of Luke-Acts "is aimed at building up local leadership so that it can strengthen the whole church *for partnership with the wandering prophets.*"[49] Luke emphasizes "a cooperative missionary effort characterized by a *fluidity in guest and host roles* [emphasis added]."[50] For instance, Paul was initially an itinerant preacher who was hosted by Barnabas.

2 7

In the language of hospitality, Barnabas welcomes the fringe Christian Paul into the mainstream of the church's life. When this volatile newcomer proceeds to make himself just as unpopular in Jerusalem as he had been in Damascus and must retreat to his home in Tarsus to escape assassination (Acts 9:28–30), Barnabas once again takes up his cause.[51]

By the end of Acts, Paul had become "both itinerant and resident, guest and host, minister of the word and minister of the table."[52] This fluidity of roles meant that the community welcomed and permitted itself to be constantly instructed by charismatic individuals from within and beyond its boundaries.

When a charismatic individual spoke a Word that was meant for the congregation, it was welcomed as potentially significant in the community's task of discerning the truth of the gospel. Even when these charismatic individuals preached a message contrary to the gospel (the law-observant evangelists at Galatia or the hedonists at Corinth) their message was allowed to be heard and was engaged in debate. This was permitted because the truth of the gospel was experienced as universal and dynamic, emerging each day in open dialogue and debate. Truth was not narrow and exclusive, identified solely with one voice, one interpretation, or one leader. For this reason, also, the church saw fit to canonize the voices of many evangelists with often conflicting agendas.

The early church, therefore, allowed for a dynamic interplay between charismatic authority and the traditional authority of hospitality.[53] There seems to have been no hierarchy between these two forms of authority. Paul's charismatic authority was not given more status than the authority of his many hosts. Paul and the leaders of the house churches shared a "bipolar authority" through which they mutually interacted for the upbuilding of the community of faith (see Philemon).[54]

When searching for images from the New Testament for the preacher, homileticians have usually focused more attention on images that undergird itinerant and charismatic forms of authority in the pulpit, especially the images of herald, messenger, and witness. It may be more helpful, however, for parish-based, congregation-centered preaching to look to Barnabas and Phoebe, or Philologus and Julia,[55] rather than to Jesus or Paul, for an image of the empowering authority of the preacher within the Christian community. The contemporary parish preacher could see the preaching ministry, at least in part, as an act of hospitality. The preacher is a *host* who welcomes to a roundtable strangers who bring various gifts into the community. As an itinerant preacher who has taken up residence, the parish preacher has, as well, a charismatic form of authority and brings a strong kerygmatic Word that must be communicated. All with a Word to share, however, are welcomed by the host and included at the roundtable, where they are placed into dialogue so that the Word of God for the community might be discerned.

The roundtable of proclamatory discernment and the Lord's table of spiritual nourishment are coextensive. The table is at the heart of Christian hospitality. Part of the host's role is to keep the pulpit and the Lord's table in as close proximity as possible. Indeed, the highest symbolic expression of the communal Word of God in preaching is the celebration of the Lord's Supper. The Table of the Lord is a sign that God is present in and through the communion of very different persons who share Christ's body and blood.

As a host at this table, the preacher is the steward of both the story of Christ and the tradition of the community. The preacher sees to it that all conversations and sacramental actions are centered on the saving work of Jesus Christ and on the mission of the church. Hosting, therefore, is both a liturgical and ecclesial act in which all are welcomed to the pulpit-table of Jesus Christ.

CHAPTER 2

Toward a Collaborative Homiletic

In recent years, many preachers have abandoned traditional forms of preaching for inductive or narrative approaches. I identify in this change a clear shift toward empowering forms of preaching and congregational leadership.

It is probable that homiletical theory will not continue to travel in the direction of inductive and narrative forms. There are already indications of a trend to restore traditional models of preaching. As preachers feel themselves beckoned to return to traditional homiletics, however, we recall some of the reasons that these models were questioned in the first place. Instead of returning to a form of preaching that is problematic, there is still room to move forward.

In order to chart the course toward collaborative preaching, I will analyze both traditional (sovereign) and more recent inductive approaches to preaching using the three criteria for nutritive empowerment established in the previous chapter: (1) face-to-face relationships, (2) participative roles, and (3) interactive persuasion.

Sovereign Preaching

Perhaps the most basic type of pastoral leadership that developed in the history of the Church is one described by

Bernard Swain as "the sovereign style."[1] By sovereign, he means that the leader embodies the point of final decision within the congregation, whether that person has actually unilaterally made these decisions or not. No matter what the situation, authority centralizes in a single person. "The buck stops here," said Harry Truman.

Sovereign models of preaching have a long and venerable history extending from the time of the prophets who interpreted the oracles of the Urim and the Thummim.[2] The sovereign preacher was the living oracle of God, the "privileged speaker"[3] who mediated God's Word to the community. In New Testament times Paul concluded that he was simply an empty conduit through which God's Word passed on its way to the hearers (I Cor. 1:17; Gal. 1:11-12; Col. 1:26). The Reformers, especially Martin Luther and John Calvin, maintained that when the preacher speaks, God speaks. According to Luther:

> God's Word is the same Word and just as much God's Word which is preached and read to prodigals, hypocrites, and the godless as to truly pious Christians and the godly . . . and . . . the preacher of the Word . . . is not the man, but it is God's Word, voice, cleansing binding and efficacy. We are only the tools, fellow-workers and helpers of God, through whom God works and executes His work. . . . We conclude thus: God Himself preaches, threatens, punishes, frightens, comforts, baptizes, administers the Sacraments of the Altar, and absolves.[4]

In the twentieth century, sovereign preaching is closely associated with the teachings of Karl Barth. Barth asserted emphatically that God speaks in human words in the act of preaching. For Barth, any "speaking of God" inevitably leads to the point where God actually speaks.[5] Many other homileticians and theologians have spoken eloquently in support of this sovereign role of preaching in the congregation.[6]

Hierarchical Relationships

Instead of promoting face-to-face relationships, a sovereign style from the pulpit suggests that people in the congregation relate to their preacher as members of a spiritual hierarchy. There are at least two aspects of the experience of hierarchy in preaching. First, the congregation is placed in a position of dependence and submission. Calvin, for instance, emphasized that hearers must learn to be completely submissive to the teaching they hear from the pulpit:

> When we come to hear the teaching that is declared to us in the name of God, we must be prepared in humility and fear to receive all that is said to us and to give heed to it and not to bring a spirit of gall, a spirit full of rebellion or arrogance or pride; but let us know what we have to do with our God, who wishes to test the obedience and subjection that we owe him. (Harmony of the Gospels: Sermon XXIV. CO 46. 286/28-38)[7]

By God's grace the congregation can overcome their own "rebelliousness, apathy, and arrogance in favor of God's teaching and call."[8]

Second, a sovereign style communicates that relationships are built on emulation, obligation, and obedience.[9] In the early church this resulted from the influence of patriarchy on leadership styles. Elizabeth A. Castelli, in her book *Imitating Paul: A Discourse of Power,* shows how the process of imitation was central to Paul's understanding of human relationships within the church. In many respects the early church was structured by "model-copy" forms of relationship. This was a by-product of the traditional familial authority accorded to the father. The child was obliged to show the father honor, obedience, and imitation.[10] In 1 Corinthians 4:14-16, Paul says:

> I am not writing this to make you ashamed, but to admonish you as my beloved children. For though you might have ten

thousand guardians in Christ, you do not have many fathers. Indeed, in Christ Jesus *I became your father* through the gospel. I appeal to you, then, *be imitators of me.* [Emphasis added]

The primary result of a hierarchical relationship between the preacher and the hearer is a centralized view of the authority of both preaching and Scripture. Members of the congregation listen to the preacher, expecting to hear the veritable Word of God. They approach preaching with humility and a clear expectation that through the guidance of the Holy Spirit, God will speak a Word to them.

The missing element is an appreciation of the identity and experience of the hearer. In a hierarchical relationship hearers do not *have* an identity and a form of religious experience; these are *given* to them by the preacher. The word spoken by the privileged speaker is supposed to either *transmit* these to the hearer, or *enculturate* the hearer over time into conformity.[11]

The face-to-face appreciation of the listener as *other* is lost in sovereign preaching. Typically the hearer's particular experiences (of gender, race, economic status, various traditions, etc.) are of little importance in the formulation of the preached message. Experience must conform always to a yet higher authority in the hierarchy of God/Scripture/Church (dogma)/preacher/congregation. This means that the monolithic Word of the preacher can constrict the unique understandings and experiences of the gospel that are already present in the congregation and usurp the congregation's power to discern, interpret, and practice the Christian faith.

The Word as Mandate

In sovereign preaching the transforming Word that guides the congregation is a decisive judgment or mandate. The Spirit of God reveals this judgment to the preacher who in turn delivers it to the congregation as a messenger. T. H. L.

Parker, in his book *Calvin's Preaching*, notes that for Calvin "the message of Scripture is sovereign, sovereign over the congregation and sovereign over the preacher."[12] In the God/Scripture/preacher/hearer hierarchy of relationships, God literally "presides as judge"[13] holding the keys to bind and to loose in heaven and on earth (Matt. 18:18). According to Parker:

> The Reformers all interpreted the power of the keys as the Church's preaching. . . . The 'legate of Christ' is the preacher. The 'mandate of reconciliation' is the Gospel. . . . Because the Gospel preached is God's Word, this is the verdict of God himself from, so to say, his judgment seat the pulpit.[14]

For the sovereign preacher the preached Word has transforming power in the community of believers because through the activity of the Spirit it becomes the final Word or Mandate of the ultimate Judge. The Word arrives as a decisive ruling or declaration that makes definitive claims on the congregation. The preacher, therefore, carefully examines Scripture for these transforming Words that will exert redemptive power within the congregation. The preacher decides on behalf of the congregation what these transforming Words will be and is assured that through the guidance of the Holy Spirit these words will accomplish a saving purpose among those who hear and obey.

This understanding of the Word of God in preaching increases prophetic and evangelical *efficiency*.[15] The transforming Word can change quickly to meet new situations as they unfold. Because the preacher, under the guidance of the Holy Spirit, determines the transforming Word on behalf of the congregation, the time-consuming, cumbersome deliberations that would be involved in a mutual process of discernment are not required.

By failing to give hearers a role in the discernment of the preached message, sovereign preaching loses much of its ability to empower congregations. As we have already noted, preaching empowers when preachers and hearers become partners in both the discernment and communication of God's Word. The interpretations of the Word that are already and everywhere present within Christian congregations are voiced in the actual language of preaching itself. Sovereign preaching prevents members of the Christian community from being included in the sermon preparation process. Thus the role of the hearer in sovereign preaching must be reconsidered, giving the hearer a more active role in the discernment and communication of the preached message.

Persuasion by Assertion and Defense

Sovereign rhetoric is the rhetoric of assertion and defense. Whether the "plain speech" of Calvinist exposition or the eloquent speech of Ciceronian oratory, sovereign rhetoric has the quality of great centering words that boldly identify evil and good, sin and salvation, falsehood and truth. Persuasion, in the sovereign form, is a function of the desire in the hearer for fixed, final, and objective truth and of the preacher's ability to tap that desire.

Assertive language is clear and precise. Because decisive judgments are at stake, the preacher is worried about being misunderstood or misconstrued. Therefore, the preacher learns to use rhetorical tools that heighten clarity, especially repetition, contrast, introductions and conclusions, deductive logic, emphasis, transitions, stock patterns, supportive data, examples, models, explanations, and comparisons.

At times sovereign preachers must defend assertions as objective truth. When this is the case, the preachers use the rhetoric of *argumentation* in order to refute competing views. They appeal to backing from Scripture, tradition, experience, and science in order to support particular truth claims. They argue for the consistency and coherence of certain ideas and test their ideas for viability, validity, and adequacy to the full range of Scripture and experience.

Sovereign forms of persuasion communicate clarity and precision of thought regarding ideas, purposes and goals. Even when the preacher's understanding of the Word of God does not match those of hearers, this form of persuasion has a way of bringing out the commitments of everyone in the congregation. When a preacher boldly asserts a definitive truth claim, hearers must ask themselves, "Do I really think that?" The preacher's assertiveness tends to bring out the assertiveness of those in the congregation who are given to opinions, either in unity with or in debate against the preacher. This makes the issues of clarity and precision of thought important within the community, even though it usually bypasses those whose minds are not already made up.

Another more positive result of sovereign persuasion is that it can promote social cohesion and a heightened sense of communal identity once the beliefs of the preacher and the hearers become a near match. Sovereign forms of persuasion can increase the congregation's commitment to a particular set of beliefs and to certain important actions. In terms of leadership, zones of stability are established in the congregation so that the preacher/leader can choose a variety of means for bringing about change.

Sovereign persuasion, however, can easily become coercive, especially when it is wielded by judgmental personalities. Those who resist coercion will react and either "go underground" or leave the community. Where agreement is reached, a kind of herd psychology can develop within the congregation about certain ideas or issues. In a congregation that agrees with them, sovereign preachers often become so self-assured that they preclude new information or arguments that represent contrary positions. When this happens, sovereign preachers—and their congregations—can become willfully naive and even irrational, riding on the crest of their own self-certainty, away from the reach of all possible critique.

Another problem is that by appealing to the hunger in the hearer for fixed, final truth, this form of persuasion can turn the Word in upon itself so that it appears only in sedimentary, substantive assertions. Instead of looking for new words that God's Spirit might desire to communicate, the preacher/leader settles for rehashing or repeating older, timeworn messages.

Rethinking Sovereignty

Sovereign leadership and sovereign preaching have come under severe criticism as potentially, if not inherently, authoritarian. The basic problem with sovereign approaches to leadership and preaching is the failure to adequately represent the servant charisma, hospitality, and mutuality that are fundamental to an empowering Christian ministry.

At least four problematic tendencies are associated with sovereign styles of preaching and leadership: (1) the tendency to deny the relevance of the hearer's experience in critically responding to the sovereign Word, (2) the tendency of "direct inspired utterance" to preclude communal interpretation of the Word, (3) the tendency of assertive rhetoric to become coercive rhetoric, and (4) the tendency to foreclose on God's transforming Word as fixed and final and to deny that this Word may change in new contexts.

In recent years congregations are attracted by a more mutual vision of the church, commensurate with the one envisioned by Paul in Galatians 3:28 in which "there is no longer slave or free, there is no longer male and female; for all of you are one in Christ Jesus." Without denying the significance of authority and leadership in the church, there is a growing concern that congregations live into a vision of the church that transcends the hierarchical limitations in which the early church attempted to live out the gospel.

Letty Russell has provided a helpful reassessment of the experience of sovereign leadership in the context of the early church. According to Russell, sovereign leadership was always qualified by the way that God's sovereign activity was expressed in Jesus Christ who "emptied himself, taking the form of a slave" (Phil. 2:7). This means that within the Christian community, sovereignty is best expressed as what Russell calls "temporary inequality" rather than as a dominant, ongoing leadership style.

> The gifts of the Spirit are not distributed equally and there is no way of reaching a static form of equality in all aspects of the life of a partnership (I Cor. 12:12-31). What is possible is the practice of *temporary inequality*. This is the sort of image that Paul uses of God's action in Jesus Christ in Phil. 2:1-11. The basis for unity is not equivalence but rather the willingness of Christ to become a servant. In our own relationships there are times when we are temporarily unequal, not by assigned status or role, but by willingness to accept this relationship for the sake of growth of the whole. Such a relationship would be that between teacher and student, parent and child, chairperson and member.[16]

Hierarchy in the church should only be *provisional*, rooted in protocols agreed upon by the congregation or the expressed desire by members of the congregation to receive instruction from those with particular forms of expertise or experience. *Hierarchy should not become a fixed form of leader-follower relationship in the church.*

Along with this rethinking of leadership, preaching has undergone significant reassessment in recent years to recapture something of the mutuality that is crucial for the leadership of the church. It is to this subject that we now turn our attention.

Dialogue and Inductive Preaching

After World War II there was growing concern to understand and disarm authoritarian leadership styles.[17] As a result, church leaders began to discuss and practice more mutual, consultative approaches to leadership.[18]

As preachers, homileticians, and theologians reflected on the problem of authoritarian pulpit leadership, they suggested many changes. Some appealed for more pastoral self-disclosure and authenticity in the pulpit.[19] Others appealed for the inclusion of the actual needs of hearers more directly in sermons.[20] Pastoral psychologists informed homileticians that sermons should promote mental health instead of irrational prophetic delusions.[21] Pastoral theologians reemphasized the importance of knowing the congregation and earning trust, respect, and love as a prerequisite for effective preaching.[22]

The image and personality of the preacher were also items of concern. Preaching was seen more readily as a symbol of authority and of the "cultural conscience" of the congregation. Preachers were warned that they could unwittingly magnify "residual feelings of guilt and inadequacy" when this symbolic role was misused.[23] Some psychologists studied the personality types of preachers, creating various typologies to help preachers understand their problematic tendencies.[24]

These critiques magnified the weaknesses of sovereign preaching and suggested the need for alternative homiletical models which would demonstrate that the thoughts and experience of the hearer had been consulted prior to preaching. Theologians, biblical scholars, and homileticians returned to the Bible in search of ways of communicating that would include the hearer in a more significant role. They unearthed a diversity of forms of communication in the Hebrew Bible and in the New Testament, especially dialogue, parable, and story.[25]

The initial result of the backlash against authoritarianism in the pulpit was the short-lived dialogue preaching movement in the 1960s.[26] Some preachers began to experiment with two-party dialogue sermons, postsermon feedback sessions, involvement of laity in sermon exegesis, removal of manuscripts and pulpits, and walk-around sermon delivery.

Dialogue preaching, however, failed to gain a significant foothold in the churches. There were several good reasons for this. In some instances preachers were insensitive, even authoritarian, in the ways that they introduced dialogue preaching in their congregations. Congregants were suddenly confronted by a preacher walking up and down the aisles "self-disclosing" within inches of their faces. Sometimes two-party dialogues exasperated congregations by appearing contrived and exclusive. While two preachers engaged in a staged dialogue, members of the congregation felt as if they had been sent offstage and were merely overhearing a pastoral conversation. Feedback sessions often became gripe sessions or back-patting sessions. Little effort was made to include feedback in forthcoming sermons.

The most significant problem, however, was the failure to discern the precise nature of dialogical speech. How could preachers transform the actual principles of dialogue into the nuts-and-bolts of homiletical practice? Given the monological character of preaching, what would the language of dialogue sound like in a sermon? What kinds of logic and rhetoric would be inclusive of the experience and thoughts of the hearer?

It was initially Fred Craddock who provided at least one important answer to this question. Craddock, in his landmark book appropriately entitled *As One Without Authority*, asserted that:

> in dialogue what one says is not fully predetermined but is in a large measure in response to the preceding comments of the other. The words are never all present at once as in a printed

text; on the contrary, words as sound move toward a goal as yet undetermined. . . . Thus there is in the act of speaking a consciousness of movement, change, uncertainty, openness to interruption, and, of course, insecurity.[27]

According to Craddock, dialogical speech should include three elements: spontaneity, open-endedness, and "revealing . . . more than was intended."[28] Craddock thought that the form of logic that best carried the freight of these dialogical elements was *inductive* logic which "moves from the particulars of experience that have a familiar ring in the listener's ear to a general truth or conclusion."[29]

Craddock insisted that the preacher should never simply present the hearer with conclusions arrived at in the minister's study. In the pulpit, the preacher should "retrace the inductive trip" taken earlier "and see if . . . hearers come to that same conclusion."[30] The open-endedness of inductive logic permits hearers to arrive at their own conclusions having made the same inductive journey taken by the minister. Craddock wants preachers to preach so that "the listener completes the sermon."[31]

Fundamental to Craddock's inductive approach is the use of identification and analogy. The inductive preacher cultivates an analogical imagination and becomes someone "who receives and shares the authentic signals of life as the congregation knows it. . . . "[32] Through identification, the preacher consults the lifeworld of the hearer for experiences that can be incorporated into the sermon in a movement toward a general conclusion.

The narrative preaching supported by Eugene Lowry in his classic book *The Homiletical Plot* is essentially a variation on Craddock's inductive model. In both instances, instead of beginning with conclusions, the preacher uses a form of logic that *delays* the arrival of the preacher's ideas. Craddock's form of delay is a series of spontaneous, experiential digressions that move toward a general conclusion. Lowry's form of delay is a series of narrative detours that arrive at an "experience of the Gospel."[33]

Inductive and narrative preaching have gone a long way toward overcoming some of the problems associated with sovereign preaching. They represent an important attempt to include the hearer in a more significant role in the preaching process.

Symmetrical Relationships

Inductive and narrative approaches moved preaching one step closer to expressing face-to-face relationships. This was accomplished by making *symmetrical* forms of preacher-hearer relationships central to the task of preaching. According to Jackson Carroll, "in symmetrical authority relationships, power within an organization such as the church is, in principle, available to all members."[34] Inductive preaching accomplishes this in part by permitting hearers to arrive at their own conclusions. The actual production of a sermon's message includes hearers and their experiences. By using the logic of joint problem solving, the preacher and hearer are in principle placed on equal ground in pursuit of clues to the solution of common problems.

Relational symmetry is undergirded in inductive preaching by one fundamental premise: that the preacher can and must *identify* with hearers. By using a kind of empathetic imagination the preacher discovers the kinds of shared experiences necessary to move inductive sermons along a common pathway to general conclusions.[35] When the preacher identifies with hearers it demonstrates that there is a symmetry of knowledge and experience between the preacher and the congregation. Because identifications are made, preacher and hearer are able to take the same "inductive trip."

Symmetrical preacher-hearer relationships are built on shared experience and expectations rather than on duty and obedience. Inductive preaching communicates that the preacher trusts the experience, abilities, and vision of those in the pews. The high value the preacher places on what the hearer brings to the preaching process is suggestive of trust in other areas of church leadership. Instead of imitating or obeying leaders, hearers are invited to experience a profound "interchangeability" between themselves and their preachers.[36] Rather than promoting dependence on the preacher, this sponsors a sense of *interdependence*.[37] Inductive preaching says that "we are all in this together." This helps to create possibilities for the experience of solidarity and partnership in the congregation.

In symmetrical relationships, however, what is often missing is the sense of how *different* the experience of someone else may in fact be. The urge for symmetry can preclude the experience of the other as truly *other*. When this is the case, the preacher easily overlooks either the unique gifts of those who seem similar to the preacher yet are, in reality, very different, or the unique gifts of those on the margins who are clearly very different from the preacher.

Preacher-hearer identification assumes that there is a common concern between all parties that can be reached in a kind of "fusion of horizons" in the preaching event.[38] This assumption creates an *ideal* symmetrical situation that disregards actual differences: a disregard that can easily become a profound disrespect for the otherness of the varied hearers in the preaching process. In other words, the assumption that the hearer is "like me" may preclude the realization that the hearer can be (temporarily) " 'above' me—not as partner but as teacher."[39] Both the temporary inequality of the preacher and the temporary inequality of the hearer can be sacrificed in inductive preaching.

The Word as Insight

In inductive and narrative preaching the Word of God is not asserted by the preacher as a decisive judgment made on the hearer's behalf. Rather, the Word presents itself as hard-won *insights* that hearers arrive at on their own during the course of the sermon. During the preaching event, the arrival of the Word is delayed by various experiential images or narrative devises of plot. The Word is anticipated and then, within the field of that anticipation, it presents itself to the hearer. In other words, this kind of preaching *invokes* the Word, it does not *tell* it.

To those in the congregation, this dynamic communicates that the discernment of God's Word for the community is a creative process instead of a matter of obeying commands and mandates. Congregants learn to puzzle over deep conflicts and to listen for the Spirit to provide words of insight. They learn that it is often necessary to go beyond the frame of a problem in order to discover creative solutions.[40]

Inductive and narrative preaching approaches also communicate that the discernment of God's Word for the Christian community is a radically plural phenomenon. The shape that the transforming Word takes for one person is not necessarily the same as it will be for another. When hearing an inductive sermon, each person's insight will be different.

The plurality occasioned by inductive and narrative preaching is a mixed blessing. On the one hand it supports a great diversity of Words within the life of the community. On the other hand it presents the problem of how to efficiently coordinate and focus these Words in order to achieve common ends. The Word occurs in preaching as a radically individual phenomenon. Although preacher and hearer arrive at insights within the same general horizon of meaning, these insights are still primarily the separate insights of discrete individuals. Unified commitments are less important than unique personal insights.

Whereas sovereign preaching foregoes communal discernment of the Word for the efficiency of individual prophetic discernment, inductive preaching foregoes communal discernment for the creativity of multiple individual insights.

Neither sovereign nor inductive forms of preaching, therefore, adequately address the need for a genuinely communal approach to discerning and articulating the truth claims of the gospel in preaching.

Persuasion by Problem Solving

Induction and narration move closer to interactive forms of persuasion by using logics of mutual problem solving. Sermons are energized by a problem, a dis-equilibrium, a search, or an enigma.[41] Something is wrong and needs fixing, something is out of balance and needs restoration, something is missing and needs to be found, something is confusing and needs to be clarified.

Literary critic Roland Barthes suggests that there are three major rhetorical devices typically used to delay the arrival of a solution to a problem.[42] The first of these devices is the *jam*. A jam (like a traffic jam) is the worsening of a problem. The preacher takes time to analyze and acknowledge the depth and breadth, the apparent insolubility of the sermon's central problem. How is this problem experienced? What are its logical and practical consequences?

The second device is the *snare*. A snare is what is commonly known as a "wild goose chase" or a "straw man." It is a false solution, an imposter who we know from the start only masquerades as hero. The preacher snares the hearer by examining possible solutions, perhaps even settling for the time being on one promising option.

A third device is the *clue*. A clue is a glimpse of what is significant in resolving the problem at hand. Eugene Lowry calls this "the homiletical 'aha' " which arrives as a reversal that "turns things upside down" or brings about a "radical change of direction" in the sermonic plot.[43] Sometimes, especially in inductive preaching, this clue takes the form of a resolving image. Instead of "telling" the congregation the solution to the problem, a story is told or an image is created in which clues to a resolution are rehearsed. Hearers, therefore, are permitted to draw their own conclusions.

One gain of this kind of preaching, as we have already seen, is that it involves the hearer in the preacher's homiletical journey and in the arrival at a homiletical destination. Robin Meyers has called this form of persuasion "self-persuasion."[44] Problem solving is the rhetoric of engagement and involvement—important dynamics where leadership is committed to deepening the experience of partnership in the church.

Another gain is that solutions to problems *often come from beyond our usual frame of reference.* They reverse the *status quo* and seem to strike hearers from outside their normal frame of reference. This is important in leading a congregation into deeper experiences of the power of the Spirit in order to provide criteria for living that transcend norms and traditions.

The most significant weakness of problem-solving rhetoric is that it can be manipulative. This leadership style is merely consultative.[45] The preacher consults the hearer's experience for images and examples to bolster an already decided upon general course of action. Like a good car salesperson, the preacher gets the hearers on the hook by showing them the car, then lets them drive the car before buying. The preacher empathizes with the hearer's feelings and experiences but still makes ultimate decisions about sermon topics and how the homiletical journey should proceed. The spontaneity and partnership of truly participatory dialogue is lost. Instead of actually participating in the sermonic process, the hearer is simply being brought along on a preestablished homiletical trip.[46]

Conclusions

Inductive and narrative forms of preaching have gone a long way toward establishing a modest form of mutuality in the pulpit. Three important issues, however, remain to be addressed. First, there is the problem of genuinely including the voice of the other (those other than the preacher). Although symmetrical relationships and identification with hearers help to restore trust and interdependence to preacher-hearer relationships, they can also do violence to real dialogue in preaching which is built on coming to terms with the other *as truly other.*

There are also the complementary problems of plurality and individualism that accompany the idea that God's Word arrives in preaching as discrete insights. While multiple spiritual insights are more creative and inclusive than single oracular mandates, the need for a more communal approach to discerning and articulating the Word of God in preaching remains.

Finally, there is the problem of achieving a thoroughly mutual form of persuasion. Although inductive problem solving language involves the hearer in the homiletical journey, this involvement is still more consultative than participative in nature. We return, then, to the same problems that plagued Fred Craddock in 1971. Since preaching is essentially monological, how best can principles and practices of truly participative dialogue be incorporated? These problems challenge us to move beyond sovereign and inductive models to investigate collaborative forms.

CHAPTER 3

Collaborative Preaching

The word *collaboration* means "working together." It implies a form of preaching in which preacher and hearer work together to establish and interpret the topics for preaching. They also decide together what the practical results of those interpretations might be for the congregation. The preacher, then, goes into the pulpit and re-presents this collaborative process in the event of sermon delivery.

Conversation and Congregational Culture

"Roundtable" conversation[1] is potentially helpful in resolving the dilemmas we have noted in relation to sovereign or inductive methods for preaching. Again, I am not suggesting that preachers actually hold conversations from the pulpit or that the two- or three-party "dialogue sermon" be reinstituted. Experimental or "staged" forms of preaching attract too much attention to style and detract from congregational leadership in the pulpit. Our goal is simply to move closer to a model of single-party preaching that faithfully represents a collaborative process of sermon preparation.

Within the past ten years communication researchers have begun to study ordinary conversation. A new field of study called "conversation analysis" has been spawned to analyze the structure, content, and contexts of conversation.[2] Conversation analysts have united with ethnographers and cultural anthropologists to demonstrate how the content and style of everyday conversation provide fundamental clues to the way that people organize and make sense out of their lives. According to conversational analyst Harvey Sacks, "in every moment of talk, people are experiencing and producing their cultures, their roles, their personalities."[3]

Congregations are organizational cultures. Organizational cultures are *talking* cultures. The best way to determine what is really going on in such cultures is to be "let in" on the talk through which the culture is being experienced and produced. Change occurs in the culture when a participant exerts influence as a dialogue partner in the range of conversations that are actually taking place within the organization.

To presume that organizational cultures such as congregations are either accurately described or qualitatively changed by official sovereign proclamations of tasks, goals, or purposes is probably a fallacy. Likewise, the assumption that leader-follower consultation actually brings about participation in a process of change is often misperceived.

Conversation analysis suggests that for a congregation to be either described accurately or changed in its totality, its leaders would immerse themselves in the actual talk that is taking place throughout the institution, in halls or walkways, in meetings, in Bible studies and classrooms, in hospital rooms and at communal meals. At the same time, leaders would create roundtable conversations designed to provide opportunities for laity to interpret the gospel and make their voices heard in ways that can have an impact on the congregation's identity and mission. During these informal and formal conversations, three general questions would be asked by leaders. (1) *What* are people really talking about? (2) *How* are they speaking to one another? (3) What influence should I exert in either of these areas in order to empower people as interpreters and agents of Christian mission?

The goal of collaborative preaching is to *engage in* and *influence* the ways that a congregation is "talking itself into" becoming a Christian community. The preacher does not present sovereign declarations of the purposes and goals of the church from the pulpit (You must, or You ought), or take the congregation on an inductive journey through which certain goals or purposes can be experienced and owned. Instead the preacher collaborates with members of the congregation, galvanizing in the pulpit the actual talk through which the community, in response to the biblical message, is experiencing and producing in its own congregational life and mission.

Conversation does not necessarily imply collaboration. We cannot assume that we are working together when we are having a conversation. Conversations can be dominated by certain parties and used to reinforce divisions or hierarchical power relations within congregations. For this reason, we need to identify a form of conversation that is commensurate with collaborative leadership and the task of sermon preparation and delivery. The image of the roundtable pulpit will be used to suggest this form of conversation.

The Roundtable Pulpit

Collaborative preaching is designed to place before an entire congregation, each Sunday morning, an ongoing, core-conversation. All members of the congregation can participate in this conversation. They can do so directly, by signing up to join the sermon brainstorming group (the sermon roundtable) or indirectly, by providing feedback to someone who is currently a member of this group. Preaching, therefore, reproduces this ongoing roundtable conversation so that the congregation can overhear its own struggle to interpret and respond faithfully to the gospel of Jesus Christ.

The image of the roundtable implies at least five things that are crucial for collaborative preaching.

1. The preacher as host

The preacher is a host who opens access to the pulpit to those whose interpretations and experiences may be very different. The preacher listens, reflects, argues, and agrees, satisfied all the while to be the "last" instead of the "first" at the roundtable to receive and communicate the divine Word.

2. A communal event

Roundtable conversations are *communal.* Although everyone cannot be bodily present in the pulpit at the same time, the roundtable pulpit includes over a period of time the voices of most participants in the life of the congregation. The voices of those who are established and those who are marginalized meet at the roundtable. Beyond the voices of present-day individuals and groups, the roundtable pulpit includes voices from the community's past, from Scripture, tradition, and congregational heritage.

3. No privileged voice

At the roundtable, all voices are equally valued. Although there will be moments of temporary inequality during which those in conversation tap the special wisdom of certain conversation partners, there is ultimately no privileged voice at the roundtable pulpit.[4] Chuck Lathrop's poem entitled "In Search of a Roundtable" puts it this way:

> Roundtabling means
> no preferred seating,
> no first and last,
> no better, and no corners
> for "the least of these."[5]

4. An open process

Roundtable conversation is open-ended. Roundness means that there is no closure to the homiletical conversation. Week by week, the homiletical conversation spirals inward and outward to include the constantly changing ideas and insights of those seated at the table. The Word of God is dynamic and emergent in nature. Although participants are guided to "come to terms" with the gospel, there is no final or complete interpretation of the gospel. Roundtable pulpit conversation keeps going around and around the table. It does not stop, though its participants may change. In this way, it captures the dynamic, creative quality of the emergent Word of God in Christian community.

5. A process with a purpose

Roundtable conversation has a purpose. It is not simply empty chatter. Something important is "on the table." The church should be guided and led. A Christian vision must be articulated. Practical decisions are to be made about the congregation's ethical commitments and mission. The round-table pulpit, therefore, has the quality of an important meeting during which the meaning and direct implications of the gospel for the congregation are being proposed.

Asymmetrical Relationships

According to conversation theory, conversations are driven by our differences, no matter how small these differences may be. Collaborative preaching takes advantage of this principle and assumes that *asymmetry* in the form of temporary inequality is the bedrock of face-to-face communication.[6] In any conversation, there are constant shifts of leadership in which there exist at least implied asymmetries of knowledge, resources, or experience.

This does not mean that collaborative preaching ignores ways in which people in conversation are alike or live within similar horizons of meaning. Identifications between conversation partners are very important for establishing common grounds for communication. Identifications, however, are only brief plateaus within the dynamics of the homiletical conversation. Differences are what start the conversation and what keep the conversation going.

This means that roundtable pulpit conversations are never really over. The fact that we are different always keeps us aware of the possibility, indeed the probability, that our conversation on this or that topic must be reopened. There is always "still something else" to be discovered in our relationship and in our communication.[7]

Accentuating difference in communication should not be confused with naive forms of tolerance or acceptance in which anything goes. Often, such notions are the result of sentimental understandings of relational symmetry in which there is a deep narcissistic assumption that "we're all really the same."[8] At other times these ideas stem from a non-relational (individualistic) and amoral relativism in which "you're free to think whatever you like—it's a free world." In collaborative preaching a plurality of perspectives is necessary in order to foster a *mutual critique* that will "enlarge our moral vision."[9]

Preacher-hearer relationships in collaborative preaching are built not on honor and obedience (sovereign approach) or on trust and shared experience (inductive approach) but on justice and love. Justice is expressed as members of the congregation discover that they are equally children of God who have important insights in the interpretation of the Bible and of spiritual experience. Love is expressed as hospitality in which welcoming means more than simply hearing from others, it means living in compassionate solidarity with others.[10] The preacher places a high value on the differences that exist in the community of faith. Preachers learn to see hearers, not as subordinates who must complete assigned tasks, or as cohorts who can share a similar journey, but as beloved strangers who are welcome to instruct the entire community on how to live.[11]

In collaborative preaching, however, preachers are not only instructed by others at the table. It is essential that preachers assert their own instructive "otherness" as well. Preachers choose moments to express clearly their premises and thoughts. Otherwise the preacher would not be a presence *in the homiletical conversation,* only a referee or facilitator *of the conversation.* Preachers, as ministers of the Christian church, ensure that the homiletical conversation is rooted in the gospel story and focused on the mission of the church. They exercise leadership both by *welcoming* all followers as equals and by *engaging* them deeply *in* conversation about Jesus Christ and what it means to be a Christian in today's world.

The goal of collaborative preaching is neither a *like-minded* community of obedient clones, nor a *tolerant* community of insightful individuals. The goal is a *learning* community of deeply engaged strangers. Participants do not imitate their leaders or "fuse horizons" with their leaders, they "come to terms with" their leaders.[12]

The most significant gain that collaborative preaching brings to congregational leadership is the potential to maintain mutuality in relationships while recognizing the experience in the prophetic community of temporary inequality or provisional hierarchy. In roundtable preaching both leader and follower, preacher and hearer are given an opportunity to express *charismata* (gifts) and to encounter one another as (provisionally) "above" each other in the role of partner-teacher.[13]

The Word as Emergent Communal Reality

In collaborative preaching many persons participate in the discernment of the preached message. The transforming Word arrives, not as a decisive judgment or as a personal insight, but as an emergent communal reality.[14] Hearers discern God's word as a new reality in the Christian community that is emerging piece by piece through the give-and-take of an open, ongoing, homiletical conversation. Collaborative preaching is a sort of musing process through which a transforming Word is "brought forth" into the open. This Word arrives in various forms: as a tentative commitment, a synthetic suggestion, a working hypothesis, or an "imaginative proposal."[15] It is a significant communal hunch that provokes open-ended thought, reflection, and experimentation. The Word itself remains very much "in process." It is related to the situation it seeks to provoke. As the situation changes in response to the transformative Word, a new Word becomes possible, moving the congregation into deeper forms of life as the community of the Word.

In order to embody and sustain this understanding of the Word of God in the church, collaborative preaching must be rooted in a communal process of discerning, articulating, and practicing the transforming Word of God in the congregation. The Word that is preached emerges out of an ongoing, structured interaction between Scripture, tradition, and multiple forms of experience. We will examine this process, called the *sermon roundtable,* more closely in chapter 4.

It is possible, however, to describe the role of the sermon roundtable in discerning the emerging reality of God's Word for a congregation. For example, members of a congregation that has recently been through a split or experienced some form of dissention may explore, as a part of their common talk, general themes of reconciliation. They may be discussing the need to "get together," or to "get on with being the church" or to "forgive and forget." These themes, however, are not yet the Word of God. They are simply topics and ways of speaking about these topics that are afoot in the congregation.

As they interact with the Bible and the claims of the gospel, participants at the sermon roundtable may decide to come to terms with the meaning of these topics as members of the congregation. As they do this, they begin to make tentative commitments or proposals concerning "forgiveness" or "getting together" that will be preached from the pulpit. These commitments or proposals relate these topics to the biblical revelation and to the *reality* of their actual situation, and become the preached Word of God for the congregation.

Because this Word arises from the congregation, the congregation is accountable for responding to it. As the situation changes, this Word will also change. In this way the Word of God is constantly emerging, not as an abstract theological or biblical category, but as a reality in our midst to which we share a common commitment.

Persuasion by Interaction

Collaborative preaching embodies a participatory form of persuasion. While the sermon remains a non-interactive, single-party communication event, *it is embedded within, and re-presents an actual interactive, multiple-party communication event (the sermon roundtable)*. The sermon avoids being coercive or manipulative inasmuch as it is faithful to the collaboration and feedback that actually took place at the sermon roundtable prior to preaching.

This means three things. First, collaborative sermons must include feedback to previous messages in forthcoming sermons. Feedback must be engaged in the ongoing brainstorming that takes place at the sermon roundtable and shared with the entire congregation in sermons.

Second, preachers will sometimes permit sermons to travel in directions that the congregation wants to go instead of toward the preacher's preferred destination. The preacher may argue against this direction in the pulpit, establish the possibility of traveling on alternative pathways, or put new and important baggage on board the sermonic vehicle. Ultimately, however, the direction a sermon, or set of sermons, takes, is determined collaboratively.

Third, the language of the collaborative sermon must be what David J. Hesselgrave calls the "rhetoric of listening,"[16] a form of communication in which preachers listen to and follow hearers toward purposive but always changeable goals. This means that *the collaborative sermon must both describe and imitate in the pulpit the collaborative process of sermon brainstorming that took place during the sermon roundtable.*

As we will see in chapter 5, a myriad of new rhetorical opportunities present themselves as the preacher reflects on the dynamics of collaborative sermon brainstorming. Some of these (explored in chapter 5) are: *summoning* parties to talk, *announcing* topics, *questioning* the adequacy of experiences or interpretations, *narrating* one's story, *revising* positions, *clarifying* points of view, *interrupting* to bring in crucial information or to play devil's advocate, *qualifying* opinions or beliefs, *agreeing* with and *supporting* others, presenting *proposals* for thought or action, *projecting* future possibilities or problems, *committing* to certain projects, *instructing* in appropriate skills, *arranging* details, and *monitoring* behaviors or practices.

Collaborative preachers will not employ a single form of logic such as deduction, induction, or plot. Sometimes *entire* sermons will be ruled by only one or two of the dynamics of roundtable conversation that occur during sermon brainstorming. On other occasions, several conversational dynamics will be covered in the course of a sermon. Roundtable sermons, therefore, can focus on one interactive dynamic or can incorporate a back and forth movement between several dynamics.

The Heart of the Web

A congregation is a web of conversations. In order to focus these conversations on the gospel and the mission of the church, participants in these conversations can be included in an ongoing, core-conversation (the sermon roundtable) where the Word of God for the congregation is discerned. Sermons describe and imitate these core-conversations so that all may hear the variety of ways in which the congregation is coming to terms with the gospel of Jesus Christ. Collaborative preachers bring into the pulpit the actual "talk" through which the community articulates its identity and mission.

Collaborative preaching promises to overcome the problems we have associated with sovereign and inductive forms of preaching and to support a mutual and empowering form of congregational leadership. Collaborative preaching respects differences as well as similarities in relationships. It generates a more participative, communal process of prophetic discernment in a congregation. Finally, the collaborative sermon yields a truly participative form of persuasion in the pulpit.

Collaborative Brainstorming: A Word to Preachers

B efore instituting a collaborative form of preaching in a congregation, the leaders in a congregation are invited to prepare the way. The information in the previous chapters is provided to suggest some of the important reasons that a congregation might embark on an adventure in collaborative preaching. A change of this particular kind requires that you spend adequate time interpreting this form of preaching to church officers and to the entire congregation.

As you do this, try to be clear that this is not merely an experimental form of preaching. You do not plan to use it for a short period of time and then move on to something else. Commit yourself and your congregation to this form of preaching as your ongoing homiletical method. Let them know that the long-term fruits of this approach for the vitality of the entire congregation are far more important than its short-term impact on Sunday morning.

You may want to establish some way to evaluate the process on a regular basis, so that concerns about this approach to preaching can be communicated to you. Be sure that you describe, in detail, what will be involved practically and the results that you anticipate. If the process is to have integrity and credibility, the actual introduction of it is best pursued as a collaborative endeavor. It is to this practical business that we now turn our attention.

The Sermon Roundtable

Collaborative preaching arises naturally out of a collaborative process of sermon brainstorming. This process is the *sermon roundtable.*

Preparation

Before taking a seat at the sermon roundtable, the preacher completes a thorough study of the biblical material for this Sunday's sermon. By virtue of the preacher's seminary training or the special training provided for most lay preachers, members of the sermon roundtable will look to the preacher to provide clarifications and insights along the way, based on exegetical and theological expertise. At the sermon roundtable, the preacher also represents the history, doctrine, and current theology of the church and of a particular denominational tradition.

Hosting

You, as preacher, are the *official* host of the sermon roundtable. Before each meeting you should welcome participants. If there are new participants, remind them that the sermon for the upcoming Sunday will be based on your conversation together. Their job is to come to terms with the gospel message for their lives and for the congregation. Together, you will discuss the biblical text for this Sunday honestly and candidly.

It is not the purpose of the roundtable to provide exact language, logic, or illustrations for the sermon. The sermon will simply describe, or imitate, the dynamics of your conversation together. Make sure that everyone present knows that you will respect confidentiality in the pulpit. It is only with permission and great pastoral sensitivity that you will ever use anything verbatim, or refer thoughts directly to particular individuals in the sermon. Everything that is said, however, will be taken seriously and may be used in your sermon preparation.

The Co-host

It is necessary to appoint a co-host to handle the ongoing work of inviting new members to attend the sermon round-table, making sure that preaching texts have been given out to group members well in advance, posting meeting times, publicizing and promoting involvement in the sermon round-table, keeping a record of the names of participants, and guiding group discussions. This will save you time-consuming administrative work and free you to participate as a full part-ner in roundtable conversations.

Appoint a co-host on an annual or biannual basis. Be sure to choose someone who would make an effective group leader. At meetings the co-host is a process person, sometimes called a facilitator, and not a participant in discussions. The primary responsibility of the co-host at meetings is to guide group process, making sure that the group covers the appro-priate ground in the allotted time.

Membership

The sermon roundtable should meet weekly and include men and women of various ages, interests, and backgrounds. Care must be taken to involve those on the margins of the community as well as those who are at the center. The sermon roundtable should include not only church members and frequent visitors but also, when possible, members of the church staff. Secretaries, janitors, and other church person-nel are often arbiters of significant circles of talk in a congregation and bring perspectives that need to be heard. As they are available, include those who are part of the congregation's connectional community—denominational personnel, workers or aid recipients at mission agencies that the church sponsors, church missionaries (retired or on furlough), and others who belong within the scope of the church's ministry. From time to time, include persons who are not church members, may not even be Christians, but live or work in the surrounding community, and perceive the church and its ministry from the outside.

Membership at the sermon roundtable should be small, no more than ten at a time. This will ensure that everyone present has an opportunity to speak. Members of the sermon roundtable should change regularly, at least every four months. For continuity, however, membership should change on a rotating basis. For instance, if you have a group of ten, rotate five on and off at scheduled intervals.

There are two reasons to keep the group changing. First, by changing members regularly, you will include the perspectives of more people, and more combinations of people. The group is not able to become an "in group" that promotes a narrow set of ideas.

Second, it broadens the influence of the group. One significant result of congregational involvement in sermon roundtables is that participants learn to listen for their own input and the input of others in every sermon. This activates their interest in, and accountability for, what is said from the pulpit. As more people are included in this process, more people will learn to listen with interest to sermons, and to claim ownership for the message that is preached.

Once you have moved through the available pool of participants in your congregation, do not quit and return to another model of sermon preparation and delivery. Instead, move back through the congregation, creating different configurations of groups. In order to avoid repeating previous groups, the co-host must keep track of each group, and of rotations that have gone before.

In most congregations, members will be eager to have some real impact on the pulpit ministry. Experience teaches that involvement increases as you continue to use this approach. Some co-hosts have found novel ways to include church members and others in roundtable conversations. In one instance, a speaker phone was used to include a person in a nursing home who found it difficult to make it to meetings. In another case, a letter was sent by a co-host (well in advance) inviting responses to several biblical texts from a sister church in Kenya. The co-host can be imaginative and find many ways to enlarge the circle of roundtable conversation.

In smaller churches, the usual pattern is to convene smaller groups that stay together for longer periods of time. As a result, it takes longer to move through the available pool of persons who are able and willing to participate. Efforts to reach beyond the congregation and include members of the community also increase the possibility of new and changing groups on an ongoing basis. These efforts also increase the possibility that new persons will join your congregation.

Collaborative preaching is not only for use in small or mid-sized congregations. Larger congregations should use slightly larger groups and rotate members more frequently. This helps the process to reach out more quickly and involve members. Even though it takes longer to include all those who wish to be included, the process still empowers laity to become involved through participation and peer feedback. Even when not participating, church members are encouraged by the realization that the "grass roots" are being heard.

Publicity

Always publicize the members of the sermon roundtable in the Sunday bulletin or another prominent place. Invite members of the congregation to offer sermon feedback to these group members after church or before the next sermon roundtable meets. This helps sermon roundtable members to take ownership for what is preached, and it involves the congregation in a process of communal accountability for the preached Word.

Preaching Texts

The co-host should make sure that members of the roundtable have a list of forthcoming biblical texts well in advance. If the lectionary is used, the co-host should note which of the lectionary texts will be preached. If the members of the roundtable decide which texts to preach, they should do so at least two weeks in advance so that ample time is provided for preparation.

Members of the group should be encouraged to look at the preaching texts in advance. They may prepare to discuss these texts in any way that they desire. Do not force a regimen of homework that will detract from the spontaneity of the group's conversation. Some members will naturally read commentaries or other secondary resources prior to meetings. Others will meditate on the text devotionally or with an eye to specific issues or concerns. All of these approaches to the biblical text will render useful material for group discussions.

Group Dynamics

1. Brainstorming, not Preparation

Sermon roundtables should be free and open discussions. *Be careful that the task of sermon preparation does not hover over the group like a dark cloud.* The group's only task is to brainstorm: to reflect honestly and candidly on the biblical text in relation to their understandings of God, the Christian tradition, their own experience and the mission of their congregation. Participants are members of sermon roundtables, not sermon *preparation* roundtables.[1] They should not focus on the details of sermon preparation. This will only stifle conversation.

Make it clear to the group that brainstorming is their task and that sermon preparation will be your job.

The co-host should not write anything on a blackboard or butcherpaper. This tends to create a work environment that constricts the freedom of the group's discussion. The co-host may want to briefly outline the group process (and timing), and state succinctly the elements of conversation that you, as preacher, will be looking for (see the next section entitled Group Timing). This will be enough official task organization.

You may take notes during the meetings. With the group's permission, you may also use a tape recorder. Tape recording, however, may inhibit conversation. If this is the case, your memory of the group's conversation should be adequate.

2. Avoid Stereotyping

From time to time, advise members of the sermon round-table that it is important to avoid "putting words into the mouths" of others. If the response of someone who is not at the roundtable is absolutely necessary, it is sometimes possible to call them on the telephone to discuss this topic or pursue their actual input at a later time. Beware of the tendency to stereotype individual responses and to generate types of responses that are speculative. Participants should not assume that they know someone else's opinions unless they have actually heard those opinions expressed. Ask participants to refer, as much as possible, to specific, concrete experiences and not to generalized "typical" experiences, especially when appealing to those who are not present.

3. Listen for Side Conversations

A roundtable conversation is not over when people leave the table. Listen for "side conversations" that may take place after the group has finished. Side conversations represent the beginning of the feedback process on this week's collaboration. Some of this feedback may be helpful for your sermon. You should only use it, however, if it represents a further development of a trajectory of conversation that occurred in the sermon roundtable. If it represents a new line of argument or reasoning, ask those who are speaking to save their insights and share them with the entire group at the next sermon roundtable. Tell participants to feel free to call you or the co-host with thoughts that come to mind later. Most people will appreciate the opportunity to communicate those things that "I should have said," or things that should be communicated privately. Once again, do not use these comments in your sermon unless they are further developments of what has already been discussed at the sermon roundtable. Usually, thoughts that are privately shared are not meant for common consumption anyway.

4. Participate

As preacher, you are not only the official host of the sermon roundtable, you are also an active and engaged participant in roundtable conversations. Participate as fully and completely as possible. Don't observe and direct. Leave group process to your co-host. Share your own insights, commitments, passions, and concerns, not only as a pastor but as a person. You will discover your own conversational voice in the pulpit only as you hear yourself engaged in conversation. Be careful, however, not to dominate.

Let the co-host lead the group process entirely. If you feel that the group process should be handled differently, discuss problems with your co-host at a later time. *Never undermine the authority of the co-host by taking over the leadership of the group process during a meeting.*

Group Timing

Typically, sermon roundtables will meet for an hour and a half, once a week. Here is one way to organize the time.

Feedback/Feedforward (ten minutes)

The co-host can focus the first ten minutes of the group's time on the following questions. They are designed to help the group discern how the previous week's sermon round-table and sermon relate to this week's conversation.

1. *How faithful was last week's sermon to our group's discussion? In order to make up for what was missing, what should we be aware of as we move toward this week's sermon?*

2. *What feedback have you heard about last week's sermon that should have an impact on our thinking as a group?*

Engaging the Biblical Text (twenty minutes)

The goal of biblical interaction is to make the Scripture an active "voice" at the roundtable. This dynamic may be facilitated by the co-host in whatever way is natural, or by using the following exercises and questions:

1. *What questions do you have about the historical context, words, or authorship of this passage that you would like to have answered?*
   (As someone who has studied the historical and literary background of this text, you, as preacher, will be a resource for your group's interaction with the Bible, providing contextual information, definitions of terms, and clarifications of various details. From time to time, you will need to represent the "voice" of the text at the roundtable and be sure that the biblical text is not misconstrued or misrepresented. Try not to be overly defensive, however. Do not strike out at interpretations that do not match what you have read in commentaries.)
2. *Interact with the author of this text. What does the author seem to be saying? What do you want to say in response?*
3. *If the text is in the form of a story, interact (don't identify) with the characters. What is your response to their actions or words? What would you like to say to each character?*

4. *Interact with the language written here. What does this kind of language do to you? How does it make you feel? What responses do you have to this language?*

Engaging One Another (sixty minutes)

It is very important that participants lift their heads out of the biblical text and engage one another in conversation about their own insights, questions, experiences, and issues. This is the portion of the sermon roundtable that will be most important for the development of your sermon.

In order to facilitate this process, the co-host should make sure that this portion of the meeting covers the following five aspects of roundtable conversation: (1) topic-setting, (2) interpretation, (3) empowerment, (4) coming to terms, and (5) practice. Here are some exercises to help the co-host engage participants in conversation with one another:

1. *Topic-setting.* Topic-setting is the identification of topics for discussion. Help the group decide "what we are to talk about" in light of their interaction with the biblical text. Ask participants what they feel is most important to talk about. Again, avoid the language of sermon preparation. *Do not ask them what should be preached, or what ideas would make a good sermon.* Instead, ask them to identify important ideas or themes that they think are prominent as they reflect on this biblical text in relation to their own lives, the church, and the world around them.

2. *Interpretation.* Interpretation is the process of discerning *the meaning* of certain topics for our lives, the church, and the world in which we live.[2] Observe how the topics your group is discussing are interpreted by members of the group. Look for differences or contrasting points of view. Ask participants to talk about them. Look for similarities or convergences of opinion. Ask participants to discuss these further. Ask what questions participants have. What clarifications are needed?

3. *Empowerment.* In a conversation, empowerment means sharing the power to generate and interpret ideas. Invite those

who have not spoken to speak. Ask who is missing from the table who might have something to say. Resist dominant frames and ask if there are other interpretations. Explore feelings people have about what is being discussed. Ask for stories.

4. *Coming to terms.* Coming to terms is the process of deciding "so what." It is the group's struggle to discern what the gospel *requires of us* as Christians and as human beings. *This process should not be avoided.* At some point, members of the group should begin to come to terms with one another regarding one or more topics under discussion. See if the group can arrive at a tentative commitment that states what they are willing to believe or do in light of the discussion underway. Ask what difference the things that are being discussed could make for the church, broader community, or world. Ask what, if anything, should be done in light of what has been discussed.

5. *Practice.* Practice is the process of deciding "how to get there." It is the practical work of mapping the meaning of the gospel onto our lives and behavior. Ask what practical steps would be necessary in order to accomplish the goals suggested. What arrangements need to be made? What personnel or resources are needed, both within and beyond the church?

The co-host should not feel compelled to cover all of these aspects of roundtable conversation in some logical order. Most groups will cover two or three of these on their own. Some personalities move almost immediately to one of these aspects of conversation and are happy to stay there. The co-host's task is to observe which areas are being covered and to lead the group into areas that are missed. If, for instance, the group tends to spend all of its time setting topics and interpreting them, the co-host should try to move the group on to empowerment, coming to terms, and practice.

Review

After side conversations have subsided and group members have left, take twenty to thirty minutes on your own to review and to write up your notes. Your notes should cover each aspect of the roundtable conversation. First, note any relevant feedback that will have an impact on your sermon preparation. Second, identify any issues or problems that arose during the group's interaction with the biblical text. Finally, and most important, note the dynamics of the hour-long conversation during which group members engaged one another in conversation. In order to facilitate this process, divide your notes according to the elements of roundtable conversation used in your group process: topic-setting, interpretation, empowerment, coming to terms, and practice. Scan the conversation looking for these elements. Don't worry about getting everything in the right order. Jot down what you recall. Be sure to include information from "side conversations" that took place after the group finished. Here are some questions to help you in your note-taking.

Topic-setting

What topics were discussed?

How were new topics announced?

Who introduced what topics?

How did people follow up on one another's topics of interest?

Interpretation

What questions were asked and answered/not answered?

What clarifications were required and made/not made?

What alternative perspectives were acknowledged?

What linkages were drawn out between points of view, ideas, or experiences?

What differentiations were made between perspectives, ideas, or experiences?

What self-corrections or corrections of others were made?

How were ideas assessed for their value or merit?

Empowerment

Did anyone resist an idea or the way that an idea was presented or framed?

What feelings were explored?

What interruptions occurred and how were they received?

What stories, experiences, or jokes were narrated and what response did they receive?

Coming to Terms

What proposals were made for various forms of action or behavior?

What commitments were stated and shared/challenged?

What scenarios were projected?

What efforts were made to inspire commitment to certain ideas or projects?

What efforts were made to sustain momentum around certain ideas or projects.

Practice

What arrangements were suggested to get something done?

What instructions were given on how to do something?

What offers were made of potential personnel or resources to get something done?

What monitoring was done of things already underway in the church or community?

Try to be in touch with your co-host between sessions. Discuss any group dynamics that need attention. For instance, it may be that one category of conversation dominated your sermon roundtable. At the next meeting, your co-host may need to steer the group into other areas of conversation in order to achieve more balance.

Another common problem is the "know-it-all." If someone in the group is dominating conversation, you may need to use a conversation management tactic. One helpful tactic is to move around and around the table, allowing each person only a certain amount of time to speak.

Your sermon may focus on only one or two areas of sermon roundtable conversation or it may include the entire conversation. The sermon will pick up the *dynamics* of the conversation. It will not repeat, verbatim, what took place. You have learned from your group what to talk about (topic-setting) and one way to talk about it (interpretation, empowerment, coming to terms, and practice). In your sermon you are free to use material from your own exegetical, theological, and cultural reading to help you rephrase, reorder, and embellish particular sequences of conversation. You are also free to take certain lines of conversation further than they were developed in the sermon roundtable. Be sure, however, to be true to the topics and dynamics of the sermon roundtable as you prepare your sermon.

CHAPTER 5

The Language
of Collaboration:
What It Sounds Like

The language of the collaborative sermon springs forth from the five dynamics of roundtable conversation that we examined in chapter 4: topic-setting, interpretation, empowerment, coming to terms, and practice. This language will either *describe* the dynamic as it took place at the sermon roundtable or it will *imitate* directly one of these dynamics. Imitation means that you repeat in the pulpit the same dynamic that took place in the sermon roundtable, perhaps using some of the same language, without actually telling the hearer that what you are saying is taken from the conversation that took place at the sermon roundtable.

For instance, if someone at the roundtable said: "I wish the apostle Paul hadn't said this," you may describe this by saying, "At the sermon roundtable, one of our members expressed a wish that Paul hadn't said this." On the other hand, you can imitate this dynamic by saying, "You may wish that Paul hadn't said this." Both description and imitation let the congregation in on the roundtable conversation that produced the sermon and include them indirectly in the discussion.

Once you have finished taking notes on the sermon roundtable, you can use this chapter as a guide to help you begin to find appropriate language to describe or imitate what took place in your sermon roundtable. Take the dynamic you have observed and turn to the section in this chapter that provides examples on how to proceed. These are only meant to be suggestions. Over the course of time you will find your own language to describe or imitate what takes place at your sermon roundtable.

1. The Language of Topic-setting

Recreate from the pulpit some of the dynamics through which the biblical material was engaged when the sermon topic was set at the sermon roundtable. This lets the congregation see that a predetermined topic is not being imposed on them and that the roundtable is not a hollow exercise. Instead, the topic for today's sermon emerged through a back and forth process of group interaction about a biblical text that includes the kinds of issues and concerns that are important to them. Through the ongoing process of the sermon roundtable and its feedback mechanism, everyone in a congregation has a real opportunity to become a "topic-setter."[1]

Three basic conversational cues are most often used to establish or "set" topics in roundtable conversations.

Announcements

An announcement is a statement that declares what a topic will be within a sequence of conversation. In a one-on-one conversation, topics are announced very directly:
"I need to talk to you about . . ."
or in the interrogative form:
"Have you got a minute to talk about . . . ?"
In a roundtable conversation, announcements tend to broaden out and focus on directions that the group might explore:
"What I find interesting is . . ."

7 4

"I think . . ."
"It could be that . . ."
"Maybe . . ."
or in the interrogative form:
"What do you think about . . . ?"
"Don't you think it's unusual that . . . ?
There are dozens of ways to announce new topics in round-table preaching. You may describe in your sermon the way that announcements were made at the sermon roundtable:

Description

"Several members of the sermon roundtable felt it was
important to look at . . ."
"Members of the sermon roundtable thought that . . ."
You may imitate in your sermon some of the ways that topics were actually announced at the roundtable:

Imitation

"Let's take just a minute to look at . . ."
"Have you ever noticed . . . ?"
"While we've been talking about . . . , you may have been wondering about . . ."
"From one perspective, the crucial issue is . . ."
"We need to take time, at some point, to talk about . . ."
"The main thing we need to talk about is . . ."
"There's something here that may strike many of you as important . . ."

Summons

A summons is a set of statements that summons a particular person or persons and then justifies the summons by announcing a topic. In one-to-one conversation, a typical summons would be:
Child: Mommy. (summons)

Mother: Yes, dear.

Child: I want a cloth to clean the windows.

             (announcement)[2]

In a roundtable discussion, a summons identifies a person or group of persons as having a particular interest in a certain topic that should be discussed by the group.

"George, you probably think we need to talk about . . ."

"George, isn't it true that educators . . . ?"

When using a summons in a sermon it is usually necessary to drop proper names and appeal to the specific group of persons who represent the point of view that you are addressing at the sermon roundtable.[3] This depends on the level of formality in your worship, and whether you have permission to use someone's name from the pulpit.

Description

"We asked the young people at our roundtable whether we shouldn't talk about . . ."

"We asked the mothers at our roundtable if it wasn't true that . . ."

Imitation

"Young people, we need to talk about . . ."

"Mothers, isn't it true that . . . ?"

Following

"Following" is language that acknowledges that you are following the hearer's lead in pursuing a topic of conversation. This is an excellent way to show in a sermon more of the variety of perspectives that existed at the sermon roundtable. In a one-on-one conversation, the language of following is immediate and focused.

"A minute ago you said . . . What I think is that . . ."

"When you said . . . I began to think that . . ."

"Because you . . . , I . . ."

"So you're. . . . I guess I'll . . ."

"Then (based on what you just said) . . ."

"You mean . . . ?"

In a roundtable conversation, such language focuses more clearly on particular discussants and sometimes becomes more formalized.

"A minute ago George and Cindy said . . . I want to follow up on that and say . . ."

"When George said . . . I began to think that . . ."

"Because George and Cindy said . . . , I . . ."

"So we've decided . . . I guess I'll . . ."

"I agree with George that . . ."

Once again, depending on the formality of your worship and whether you have permission, you may or may not divulge in your sermon the name of the one who suggested the topic you are pursuing. If you use a name, ask permission and only use material that will encourage and not embarrass the person named.

Description

"At the sermon roundtable, Cindy Jones said that . . . Bob Smith followed up on this by asking if . . ."

Imitation

"Cindy Jones told me that . . . But Bob Smith asked me if this means that . . ."

It is usually more appropriate to drop proper names and to appeal to specific groups of people who may represent a point of view.

Description

"One member of our roundtable suggested that . . . We followed up on this by asking if . . ."

Imitation

"In response to the suggestion that . . . , I've heard it asked if . . ."

2. The Language of Interpretation

As topics are set, they will also be interpreted. A topic is similar to the subject of a sentence. It is what we are talking about at any given moment in a conversation. Interpretation is similar to the predicate of a sentence. It is what we are saying about what we are talking about. A topic such as "love," for instance, has had many well-known predicates. In the movie *Love Story,* love "means never having to say you're sorry." In 1 Corinthians 13, love "bears all things, believes all things, hopes all things, endures all things."

Interpretation is not an art or a science at the disposal of an interpretive elite. Roundtable interpretation occurs in the back and forth, face-to-face speaking and hearing in which the intelligibility and meaning of ideas and experiences are explored and established. There are several basic interpretive strategems that occur in roundtable conversations that can be described or imitated in the collaborative sermon.

Clarification

One way to establish the meaning of an idea is to pursue clarification. The process of clarification often involves posing questions that will ensure that group members share a unified understanding.

When using questions in a sermon, please avoid putting too many different questions back to back. If you cannot do this, be certain that each question says precisely the same thing. Otherwise, the hearer finds it difficult to discern which one requires answering. When questions are used as interpretive tools, they require at least attempted answers. Questions should never be left dangling.

You may want to identify questions that were central to the roundtable conversation:

Description

"At the roundtable, one fundamental question was . . ."
Or you can imitate the process whereby this fundamental question was asked of the roundtable:

Imitation

"How can we think about . . . ?"
"Why does Jesus . . . ?"
"What do you think about . . . ?"
Another way to go about this is to summarize a clarification that took place:

Description

"At the sermon roundtable we had to clarify the meaning of . . ."

Imitation

"Let's clarify the meaning of . . ."
Recall the way that an important question was raised in your sermon roundtable and try to capture this dynamic in your sermon.

From time to time clarification will require a teaching sequence in which "the 'egalitarian' style which characterizes informal dialogue is temporarily replaced by a 'hierarchical' one"[4] so that the group might hear from someone with a particular expertise. You may want to recognize this expertise briefly, in order to demonstrate how members of the group learned from one another.

Description

"Our roundtable asked Susan to look up the Greek word for . . ."
"Our roundtable appreciated the expertise of . . . on the issue of . . . He told us that . . ."

Imitation

"In the Greek the word . . . means . . ."

"An expert on . . . in our congregation says that . . ."

Contrapuntal

Sometimes in a roundtable conversation, it is important to take note of similar or competing interpretations without actually engaging them in discussion. This helps to clarify the position of the topic under discussion in relation to other ideas. The word "contrapuntal" was used by David Buttrick to describe a sequence or statement that "acknowledges, but does not reinforce, an opposition."[5] The preacher acknowledges alternative perspectives without arguing for or against them. If alternate perspectives were noted but avoided by your sermon roundtable, you may want to make use of a contrapuntal.

Description

"Members of the sermon roundtable were aware of other ways that this could be seen. For instance . . ."

Imitation

"There are other ways to see this, of course. For instance, . . ."

"There are complementary points of view, those of ____ and ____, for example."

"There are a few competing ideas, of course. For instance, . . ."

Linking

In most roundtable conversations, those with similar views find ways to link their interpretations with one another. This is a form of "following" that is designed to solidify a particular interpretation.[6] Attempts at linkage can either be accepted (agreement) or rejected (disagreement). Agreement might sound like this:

Description

"Members of the sermon roundtable agreed that we generally see this the same way."

Imitation

"Do we see this the same way? Based on what I have heard, I think that we do."

Disagreement might sound like this:

Description

"When it was suggested that we see this the same way, members of the roundtable generally disagreed."

Imitation

"Do we see this the same way? Some of you have told me that we don't."

Differentiation

The opposite of linkage is differentiation. Roundtable conversations often include exchanges aimed at clarifying the differences between interpretations at the table. Once again, these attempts at differentiation can be accepted (agreeing to disagree), or rejected (appeals for further negotiation). In a sermon, an agreement to disagree might sound like this:

Description

"At our sermon roundtable, we saw things very differently. Some seemed to be saying that . . . Others were saying that . . ."

Imitation

"We see this very differently. Some seem to be saying that . . . Others are saying that . . ."

An appeal for further negotiation might sound like this:

Description

"At our sermon roundtable we saw this very differently. Some said . . . Others said that . . . This appeared to be a real difference of understanding. Yet several members of the group suggested that maybe we were not so far apart on   this as it seemed . . ."

Imitation

"We see this very differently. Some seem to be saying that . . . Others are saying . . . This appears to be a real difference of understanding. Yet several of you have suggested that we're not so far apart on this as it seems."

Repair

At the sermon roundtable there will be times when members revise their interpretations based on new information.[7] This information may have come from tradition, the Bible, or from other interpreters taking part in the discussion.

Repair sometimes involves self-disclosure and may mean acknowledging a self-correction. In a sermon, this dynamic might sound like this:

Description

"At least one person at our sermon roundtable changed their mind about this and decided that . . ."

"After I heard what members of the roundtable had to say about this, I changed my mind and decided that . . ."

Imitation

"I know that several of you have changed your minds about this and decided that . . ."

"Until recently I thought that . . . But after studying this biblical passage and listening to several of you, I have decided that . . ."

Assessment

Assessment is the process of estimating the value of a particular interpretation. In a roundtable discussion, assessment is often pursued through assertions of value. Most of these are usable in sermons.

Description

"This made good sense to our sermon roundtable."
"This seemed to be a valuable idea at our roundtable."

Imitation

"I get the idea that this makes good sense to many of you."
"This seems to be a valuable idea for many people."
In cases of negative assessment, opposite forms may be necessary.

Description

"This didn't make good sense to most persons at our sermon roundtable."

Imitation

"This doesn't make much sense, does it?"

3. The Language of Empowerment

Much of the language of empowerment has been discovered and codified by psychotherapists and students of group process. The purpose of such language is, on the one hand, to empower individuals toward more responsibility for feelings and actions and, on the other hand, to enable groups to "metacommunicate" about how they are doing at the job of being a group together.

Framing

According to Deborah Tannen, people live within certain "frames."[8] Each individual has his or her own "frame of reference." Asserting the uniqueness and importance of our frames is how we get a "footing" in a conversation or how we hold on to our own footing.[9] Sometimes we are content to fit into the frames provided by others. In a roundtable conversation, however, it is important that each member be given the opportunity to both resist or change the frame for the discussion. When such language is heard, it empowers others to resist or change the frame also.

Frame Resistance

Often it is important for a congregation to experience ways that certain frames of reference were resisted by members of the sermon roundtable, especially when these frames are unjust or oppressive. Hearing a frame resisted can be empowering, especially when the frame that is being imposed is fundamentally inconsistent with the message of the gospel.

Frame resistance is sometimes accomplished by naming the frame and defining its boundaries.

Description

"Several members of our sermon roundtable felt that this was simply a psychological point of view."

Imitation

"Many of us are not satisfied to see this issue through the eyes of a psychologist."

The problem with this kind of frame resistance is that it often appears to be confrontational. It can feel dangerously close to a "put-down" that stereotypes another person into a narrow role. It also gives more substance to the frame being resisted than one might desire.[10] A better way to resist a particular frame is to "change the frame without naming it."[11]

Description

"At the sermon roundtable there was concern that other perspectives were not being considered, especially those of . . ."

Imitation

"We've spent a lot of time looking at this from this perspective. Let's see if there are other ways to look at it."

"What else is there to say that we haven't considered?"

Reframing

Often our own frames of reference are unconscious, having been built up over years of life in a particular situation. These frames may need changing in order for us to discover new ways of thinking and acting. For instance, according to J. Randall Nichols, when a therapist tells a family that a child's behavior stems from certain family patterns instead of from "badness" the family may experience a re-framing that empowers them to think and behave in new ways.[12]

At the sermon roundtable, re-framing may have come from someone who was able to see different connections and meanings that cast new light on the topic at hand.

Description

"Several members of our sermon roundtable, who were reflecting on their own experiences of grief, helped us to see that . . ."

Imitation

"From those who have reflected on their own experiences of grief comes a new way of thinking about . . ."

"There's a connection here that we may never have considered if it weren't for those who have reflected on their own experiences of grief."

Another way to accomplish reframing is to tell a story that works a reversal on our usual expectations. Just as Jesus so often told parables that shattered the expectations of the hearer, preachers can use stories to change the hearer's frame of reference on a certain topic.

Empathic Response

Another avenue to empowerment is to permit the expression of significant feelings. Rogerian psychologists taught a generation of counselors to paraphrase what they sensed to be a client's feelings about a topic being discussed. They discovered that this empowered the client to claim responsibility for those feelings and to respond to them in meaningful ways. In a sermon it may be important for the congregation to share the commitment a particular person or group has to a particular idea. Be careful not to betray confidentiality when describing feelings that were expressed at the sermon roundtable.

Description

"What I heard at our sermon roundtable was that some of us feel strongly that . . ."

When imitating this dynamic from the roundtable it is important to remember that it is extremely difficult to gain access to actual feelings, and even more difficult to avoid imputing feelings that do not exist. It is helpful, therefore, to use qualifiers such as "may" or "might" to avoid constricting the hearer's feelings from the pulpit.

Imitation

"Some of you may feel the need for . . ."
"You may feel . . ." or, more specifically:
"I understand that many children in our congregation feel strongly that . . ."

Interruption

Interruption as a force for empowerment seems like a contradiction in terms. Interruptions introduce new or anticipated material before someone else's turn at speaking has properly ended. They signal either intentional or unintentional disregard for normal turn-taking transitions in conversation in order for a speaker to "get in" on the discussion at hand, or change topics altogether.

Although interruptions are considered rude and introduce a certain amount of disorder into conversations, they can serve two important empowering purposes.[13] (1) They may enable the homiletical conversation to sustain several subconversations that can influence the final direction of the sermon. (2) They can enable voices on the periphery to interject brief qualifiers and alternative agendas that need to be heard, but which cannot get the floor in any other way. When describing this dynamic, you may want to indicate the positive function of interruption so that hearers are able to get beyond the common assumption that interruptions are simply rude.

Description

"One helpful interruption at our sermon roundtable was offered at this point to remind us that . . ."
"Several members of our sermon roundtable had to interrupt our conversation several times to remind us that . . .This helped us to see that . . ."

Imitation

"What hasn't been considered, but ought to be, is . . ."

"Let's not forget . . ."

"Keep in mind . . ."

"If you have experienced the loneliness that accompanies grief, you may feel the need to interrupt at this point to say that . . ."

"Wait a minute. I just remembered something important . . ."

Storytelling

When the concrete stories of those at the table who have experienced social marginalization, oppression, or suffering are told with reverence and respect from the pulpit, story telling becomes a means of empowerment.[14] These stories should not be sentimental stories that illustrate ideas about suffering or marginalization that are held by those who occupy positions of status and power. Rather, these stories should be told in such a way that they teach lessons that those with power may need to learn.

In a recent sermon on 2 Corinthians 4:13–5:1, Marian McClure told this story about a woman who discovered the strength and boldness in Christ to leave an abusive husband.

A woman in Massachusetts wrote about her experience of being married to a man who battered her and stopped at nothing to control her and isolate her, including manipulating the children to report on her activities. One day in her prayers, this woman was focusing on a mental image of Christ on the cross. Suddenly, the image moved from being in front of her to being beside her. She understood this to mean that Christ was not going to rescue her like a hero. Instead, Christ was suffering alongside of her and wanted her to be healthful and happy. The decision to leave was up to her, and Christ would remain beside her either way. Because her invisible, inner spiritual world was all-encompassing, Christ would be with her wherever she was. Because her life with God was not confined to a place or time of day or marital status, but was her very world, she could leave her tormenter without leaving God.

She did leave, one day when her husband was distracted in the back yard. It takes courage to leave someone who is likely to come after you in a brutal rage. It takes courage to then become an Episcopal priest, as she did. And it takes boldness to speak the good news of God's grace for battered women.[15]

This story empowers those with similar experiences to reinterpret their situation in light of the gospel. It also invites those who think that women should "stay in their place" to reexamine their understanding of the Christian message.

4. The Language of Coming to Terms

Collaborative preaching not only rehearses in the pulpit the way that members of the sermon roundtable set topics, interpreted those topics, and empowered one another to speak their mind about those topics, it also recaptures the way that members of the sermon roundtable came to terms with those topics. There are moments in most roundtable conversations when participants begin to decide what needs to be done, project a vision, indicate priorities, and inspire one another to certain forms of action. The language of coming to terms is present whenever the sermon begins to suggest those things that members of the sermon roundtable decided could be done in light of their discussion. There are four typical forms that coming to terms takes in collaborative preaching.

Commitments

One way to come to terms is to suggest tentative commitments to certain forms of action. Expressing a commitment is more a statement of solidarity than of consensus or agreement. It is the expressed willingness to act in particular ways, despite the ambiguities and uncertainties that surround such a decision.

Description

"At the sermon roundtable, a strong commitment was expressed to . . ."

Imitation

"In light of this, there is one commitment that some of us have already made."

Proposals

Another way to come to terms with others is to qualify judgments or assertions and make them into proposals for action. Proposals usually contain qualifiers such as "perhaps," "maybe," "could," "might," "would," "in my opinion," "I think," "from my perspective," "according to . . . ," and so on. Instead of being asked to react to certain imperatives, therefore, the hearers of your sermon are invited to consider certain proposals.

Description

"One proposal that was made at the sermon roundtable was that we might . . ."
"It was suggested at the sermon roundtable that we could . . ."

Imitation

"One thing we could do is . . ."
"This indicates that we might . . ."
"Maybe we could . . ."

Projection

Projection is the articulation of possible scenarios. The preacher can describe or imitate ways that members of the sermon roundtable projected imaginative futures into which individuals or the congregation might live.

Description

"Here's what the sermon roundtable thought might happen if we . . ."
"Several members of the sermon roundtable dreamed up this scenario . . ."

Imitation

"Some of you have suggested what might happen if we . . ."
"Here's what might happen if we . . ."
"Here's one way to go."

Inspiring

A certain amount of enthusiasm should be generated in order for any project to be initiated. At the sermon roundtable, inspirational language will often be used. Inspirational language is usually the language of value, energy, anticipation, and hope.

Description

"The sermon roundtable was really excited about . . ."
"This idea seemed to energize our roundtable."

Imitation

"This seems to be a powerful idea!"
Sometimes an interrogative form will invite others to get on board.

Description

"Can you get as energized about this as our sermon roundtable did?"

Imitation

"This is really hopeful, don't you think?"

Sustaining

Some sequences of conversation are designed to sustain momentum around a current idea or project.

Description

"The members of our sermon roundtable think it is crucial that we keep . . ."

Imitation

"You've reminded me that it is crucial for us to keep . . ."

5. The Language of Practice

After deciding what needs to be done (coming to terms), the sermon may indicate how those at the sermon roundtable thought it could be accomplished. The conversation shifts toward thinking through the personnel, process, skills, and resources needed to make something happen.

Arranging

Sometimes the sermon roundtable becomes involved in arranging the details of a particular project. The collaborative sermon presents these arrangements as a potential form of communal or individual practice. Arrangements answer the question: "If we were to do this, how would we get it done?"

Description

"The sermon roundtable suggested several things that we could do together to accomplish this. For instance . . ."

"These are the practical steps I heard members of the sermon roundtable suggesting for us . . ."

Imitation

"Here's a list of things I hear us saying need to get done."
"Let me repeat back to you what has been suggested for us to do."

Instructing

Instruction goes beyond arranging what needs to happen to telling how a difficult task can be accomplished. Instruction assumes that one member of the congregation has a certain expertise or skill that needs to be taught to others. It is a response to the question: "How does someone . . . ?"

Description

"According to one expert at our sermon roundtable, in order to . . . , you first have to . . ."

Imitation

"I've been advised that the first part of the job is . . ."
"According to . . . , we first have to . . ."
"Here are the main ingredients."

Offering

In practical conversations, personnel needs are often answered by either offering one's own time or talent, or by suggesting that other people offer theirs.

Description

"Several sermon roundtable members said that they could . . ."

"Sermon roundtable members pointed out how much expertise in this area we have in our congregation."

Imitation

"Several of us have said that they could . . ."
"Some in our congregation have expertise in . . ."

Monitoring

Monitoring is the conversational process of task evaluation. Instead of handing out evaluation sheets or going through formal evaluation procedures, ongoing homiletical conversations can contain a feedback component that monitors how things are going on projects of mutual interest.

Description

"Members of the roundtable felt that things are going well with . . ."

Imitation

"I hear that things are going fairly well with . . . ?"

Learn by Listening, Teach by Doing

I have only provided a few examples of the kinds of language that occur in sermon roundtables that are useful for collaborative preaching. The best way to discover this language and learn to use it in preaching is to listen carefully during sermon roundtable discussions for ways that each of these categories of talk are present. Observe how members of a group speak to one another. See if there are any other ways of communicating that you can use in your preaching.

CHAPTER 6

A Case Study

The case study in this chapter will offer you an example of how to proceed in your sermon preparation. I make use of a sermon roundtable conversation that parallels thematically some of the ideas in this book. Before beginning, here is a brief description of the members of the sermon roundtable who contribute to the conversation for this sermon.

Joe—forties, co-host
Carl—forties, father of five, son of a missionary
Sue—thirties, lives in the neighborhood, not a church member, mother of two
Bert—thirties, single, lawyer
Jill—fifties, former missionary, mother of two
Janice—thirties, single, employed mother of three
Jim—forties, father of three, chemist
Marge—sixties, mother of three, worked at home
Bob—sixties, Marge's spouse, retired CPA
Mary—sixties, mother of two, retired pre-school teacher
John—myself, forties, father of two

The biblical text on the table is 2 Corinthians 11:21b-30; 12:7b-10.

But whatever anyone dares to boast of—I am speaking as a fool—I also dare to boast of that. Are they Hebrews? So am I. Are they Israelites? So am I . . . Are they ministers of Christ? I am talking like a madman—I am a better one: with far greater labors, far more imprisonments, with countless floggings, and often near death. Five times I have received from the Jews the forty lashes minus one. Three times I was beaten with rods. Once I received a stoning. Three times I was shipwrecked; for a night and a day I was adrift at sea; on frequent journeys, in danger from rivers, danger from bandits, danger from my own people, danger from Gentiles, danger in the city, danger in the wilderness, danger at sea, danger from false brothers and sisters; in toil and hardship, through many a sleepless night, hungry and thirsty, often without food, cold and naked. And, besides other things, I am under daily pressure because of my anxiety for all the churches. Who is weak, and I am not weak? Who is made to stumble, and I am not indignant?

If I must boast, I will boast of the things that show my weakness. . . .

Therefore, to keep me from being too elated, a thorn was given me in the flesh, a messenger of Satan to torment me, to keep me from being too elated. Three times I appealed to the Lord about this, that it would leave me, but he said to me, "My grace is sufficient for you, for power is made perfect in weakness." So, I will boast all the more gladly of my weaknesses, so that the power of Christ may dwell in me. Therefore I am content with weaknesses, insults, hardships, persecutions, and calamities for the sake of Christ; for whenever I am weak, then I am strong.

We do not have the space to transcribe the entire roundtable conversation. Instead, I have included excerpts (out of sequence) that proved to be crucial for the sermon I prepared.

Janice: I have a hard time with Christians who are boastful about what they believe.

John: I sometimes wish Paul hadn't spoken this way . . .

talking about himself so much . . . it sets a poor example.

Bob: Maybe he wishes he could tear up these words and start over.

Jim: But Paul boasts in weakness and suffering. That's really different.

Sue: I think that talking like Paul does takes a lot of chutzpah. He's not exactly a weakling here, if you ask me. He seems pretty "pumped up" on himself.

Jill: I agree. He's still trying to "go one up" on his opponents. We've all heard people who play this humility game.

Mary: Did you ever hear someone say: "I'm too good a Christian to do that! "?

Carl: Whenever preachers' kids or missionaries' kids get together, they like to talk about the servant complexes and martyr complexes that they have inherited.

Jill: I have another reason for not liking this way of thinking. It's the kind of thing a friend of mine used to say that made her stay in a bad marriage. She wouldn't leave her husband because Christians are supposed to suffer—to turn the other cheek.

Janice: I've been thinking more about this. Maybe Paul is trying to figure out the best way to talk about *Christ*. This idea of power in weakness has to come from his thinking about the crucifixion. He doesn't seem too happy to be speaking this way, anyway. But it's probably all he can figure out to say at the time. He calls it foolish, doesn't he?

Jim: I like a lot what Janice is saying. Paul was a human being like the rest of us. He made mistakes and he was struggling to figure out how to make sense out of things. After all, Jesus was pretty powerless on the Cross. Paul's probably trying to figure out Christ's weakness and how it relates to his own life.

Janice: That's funny. I never thought of God not having any power.

Bob: I've heard that idea before, and I'm not so sure that I like it. As far as I'm concerned, God has all power.

Jim: What kind of power—"superpower"? Paul is against that kind of power.

Janice: At the Cross, it looks like God gives up power, or at least identifies with the powerless. No "super-power" at the Cross!

Joe: (co-host) What do you mean?

Janice: I'm not sure I know what I mean. It's like the Bible passage, "when I was hungry, you fed me, when I was thirsty you gave me drink, when I was in prison you visited me," and so on. Christ is not the one feeding, but the one being fed.

Bob: I still don't like this idea. There are too many people today who want to take God's power away. It's the reason the liberal churches are in such a mess.

Jim: I don't hear Janice taking away God's power. . . . She's just trying to figure out what kind of power it is.

John: Maybe we're talking about two different kinds of power. Paul seems to have a different kind of power in mind, but a real power nonetheless . . . power that is found in weakness.

Joe: (co-host) What difference would this kind of power make in our lives, or in our church?

Jill: Maybe when we suffer on behalf of God's truth, or do things to help those who are suffering, we help God to have power—we become the power of love in the world. It's as if God needs us in order to have this kind of power . . . in order for love to grow. I've seen this during my years on the mission field.

Bert: Where I work, this kind of power sure wouldn't stand much of a chance. Nice guys finish last.

Joe: (co-host) What could be done to change this?

Jill: I think that the church could become a training

ground for this kind of power . . . a place where we share and give away power, in order to learn the power of love.

Bert: That really goes against the grain, though. Wouldn't we just be setting each other up for a fall, in the real world?

Jill: Maybe so . . . but isn't that exactly the foolishness that Paul is talking about?

Notes

Here are some of the notes that I took after the meeting was over.

Topic-setting

Janice announced she had a hard time with Christians boasting.

I followed this by expressing my distress about boasting and preaching.

Mary announced indirectly that the apostle Paul might have a martyr complex.

Carl followed this by indicating that this is the common plight of preachers' kids and missionaries' kids.

Jill followed up on this with the story of her friend who used this kind of thinking to rationalize staying in an abusive marriage.

Jim announced that Paul boasts in suffering, not "super-power."

Janice followed that Paul was trying to figure out Christ on the Cross . . . Christ's powerlessness . . . God's powerlessness.

Jill followed that God needs us, in some sense, in order to have power—power as love.

Interpretation

Jim wanted clarification on the nature of power.

Janice attempted to clarify Christ's "powerlessness" by referring to "I was hungry, . . ."—the idea that Christ was incarnate in the needy.

Bob disagreed that God is, in any way, "powerless."
(Bob's line of argument was not taken up by anyone in the group—it was avoided.)

Empowerment

Sue resisted the idea that Paul was, in any way, a weakling. She noticed his "chutzpah."

Jill resisted Paul's frame of reference because it can become self-victimizing.

Bob resisted the frame of a "powerless" God. He interrupted twice to announce this concern.

Bert resisted the frame of shared power. He thought it was unrealistic in today's world.

Jill reframed Bob and Bert's concerns as the reason Paul sees this way of thinking and acting as "foolishness," but nonetheless Christ's way.

Coming to Terms

Jill projected a scenario of the church as a "training ground" for this new kind of power.

Practice

There were no clear practical suggestions.

Approaching the Sermon

In my sermon I will use several of my notes and my memory of the conversational dynamics from the portion of the sermon roundtable transcribed above. I will supplement these dynamics with aspects of my own interaction with the biblical text and various other resources. However, I will let the conversation at the sermon roundtable have a primary influence on the dynamics of the sermon.

"Hindsight," as they say, "is always 20/20." Similar to many sermon roundtables, this group's discussion failed to meet my ideal expectations. For one thing, we failed to go deep enough in our discussion of the problems associated with "boasting in weakness." In retrospect, I wish we had gone further into this topic, especially as it pertains to the issue of domestic violence.

I am even more dissatisfied with our discussion of the nature of power. The movement from Paul's power to Christ's power and from Christ's power to God's power is unclear. There are many unanswered questions in our discussion of God's power. Does God have all power (in a supernatural sense)? Does God really have all power, but choose to give it up? Does God actually have limited power? How does God's "weakness" empower the church?

Lingering sovereign and inductive impulses make me want to either take one of these topics and set folks straight, or establish common horizons of meaning in which we could travel toward an appropriate set of insights about one of these topics. However, in order for the sermon to reflect what actually took place in the sermon roundtable, I must avoid these tendencies and attempt to be true to the conversation as it occurred. This means that I must trust that these issues can be given more attention in future sermons.

The Sermon

Power in Weakness

Some of you, while at our sermon roundtable for today's sermon, told me that you have a hard time with Christians who boast all the time about what they believe. Most of us here today probably know what I'm talking about.

For instance, you're struggling with issues of faith and doubt in a Bible study and somebody interrupts and boasts: "I just love the Lord so much!"

Or, you've just walked into church for the first time in three weeks and the first person you meet bends your ear for thirty minutes about what they did at church for the past month: attending Sunday school, singing in the choir, volunteering at the soup kitchen, and leading the women's association Bible study . . . .

It seems like the people Paul calls "superapostles" could even go one up on these people. They really knew how to boast, flashing their credentials and "letters of recommendation" and dazzling the crowd with "signs and wonders and mighty works."

Of course, it didn't take long for those at our roundtable to notice that Paul gets in on the act too. He jumps right in there, fighting fire with fire. He can outboast anyone, he says. He spends no less than two and a half chapters of his letter to the Corinthians boasting.

I sometimes wish Paul hadn't spoken in this way. It sets a bad example for preachers . . . standing up in front of everyone and talking about themselves . . . comparing people with themselves. It just sounds bad. I wouldn't doubt if Paul wished he could tear up these words after he had mailed his letter to the Corinthians.

But is Paul's boasting all that bad? After all, Paul boasts *in weakness and suffering*, not in his credentials, his diplomas, or the great signs or wonders he has seen. He says:

> I have received . . . the forty lashes minus one. Three times I was beaten with rods. Once I received a stoning. Three times I was shipwrecked; for a night and a day I was adrift at sea.

Paul brags about the dangers and hardships he endured. He boasts that he is the weakest of the weak. Paul was trying to put as much distance between himself and the superapostles as he could.

Have you ever noticed that for some people Christian ministry is measured by signs and wonders while for others it is measured by suffering and service? The church seems to be divided on this point.

Some people love to boast about how their minister cuts a striking figure, or breathes fire in the pulpit. But Paul boasts loud and long about the dangers he has endured. Unlike the superapostles, Paul says that he has suffered "danger from rivers, danger from bandits, danger from my own people, danger from Gentiles, danger in the city, danger in the wilderness, danger at sea, danger from false brothers and sisters . . ." This is quite a different checklist by which to do a ministerial job evaluation than the ones many people like to use.

But, as some of you have been quick to point out, there can be problems with boasting in one's suffering and weakness. After all, Paul was still trying to "go one up" on his opponents, wasn't he? We've all heard Christians do that . . . brag about their poverty and simplicity of lifestyle in order to get a leg up on someone who has more than they have. It's a kind of "sour grapes" mentality.

Your friend is talking gleefuly about his new BMW convertible and you just feel *compelled* to tell him that you are quite satisfied to hang on to your old Plymouth. That way you can give more money to charity!

When I was a kid, Christian parents were trained to think this way.

"Go ahead and take the last piece of chicken. I'll do without."

Whenever preachers' kids or missionaries' kids get together, they like to talk about the servant complexes and martyr complexes that they have inherited. Is this what Paul had in mind? Is Paul's boasting just the result of a martyr complex?

Probably not. But at least one member of our roundtable worried that a lot of people tragically misunderstand Paul when he boasts in his suffering. She has seen this kind of thinking at work with a friend who was a victim of domestic violence. What we are now learning about spouse abuse should make us worry about this kind of thing. Being great in weakness? Boasting in one's sufferings? This is the kind of thinking that makes a lot of women stay put in dangerous marriages. "I'm a Christian. How could I leave him?" How many women have thought or said that? It seems to me that we've really made a mess out of this way of thinking. A real mess.

But just how weak is Paul, really? Doesn't Paul's boasting take a certain amount of chutzpah? Paul is not exactly a weakling here, is he? He may have suffered, but he seems to find plenty of strength when he writes these blistering words to the Corinthian church. Paul isn't a passive victim of suffering. He actually does find power in his weakness, doesn't he?—power to stand up to the superapostles, power to declare that he is right and that they are wrong.

How is it that such power comes forth from weakness?

Several of you who have experienced great suffering and hardship have reminded me of something that we haven't yet considered: that Paul has his eyes on Christ when he places such a high value on suffering and weakness. After all, Paul says: "I will boast all the more gladly of my weaknesses, *so that the power of Christ may dwell in me.*"

I think that this is worth taking seriously, because identifying with the suffering and the weak is at the heart of the teachings of Jesus.

While strong people tend to stick together with those who are like them, and to be aggressive toward outsiders, Jesus tells his disciples to break with their own families and to show hospitality for outsiders and strangers.

While the strong tend to give privileges to those higher up on the ladder of success, Jesus says, "Whoever would be first among you must be slave of all."

While those who are strong show a natural preference for others who are strong and healthy, time and time again Jesus identified himself with the hopelessly ill.

It has been said that at the crucifixion, Jesus identified himself so closely with the suffering and weak that he actually took their place.

Until recently I thought that God and the word *power* meant roughly the same thing. I would have thought that it was ludicrous to say that God is powerless, or that God does not have all power, or that God does not have the kind of super-power that we usually associate with the idea of "power." Yet the more I have pondered the Cross and the more I listen to different ones of you who have suffered great pain or loss, the more I wonder if God is not powerless, in a way. Could it be that in some sense, God is not "an independent and self-sufficient power above the world, but is the needing and powerless One among us . . . ."[1]

I realize that this goes against the grain of our usual way of thinking. Members of our sermon roundtable were not entirely happy with this way of thinking. It sounds like foolishness to us when we think of some of its implications. After all, doesn't a weak God mean a weak church? Paul found himself feeling like a "madman" as he boasted in his weakness. He sounds as surprised as anyone that God's power might be revealed at precisely the point where God gives up everything we ever thought of as "power."

It was suggested at our roundtable that part of the power of the Cross may be *the power that the Cross calls forth in each of us.* It is as if God was saying at the Cross that God needs and waits for our response. It's as if God is, to a certain extent, *dependent on us* in order to have redemptive power in this world.

This would be a real change for many of us . . . to quit seeing God as having potentially miraculous powers over us, a "super God" with "superapostles." It would be an even greater change to see God as depending on us to complete God's power, to do something that will bring about redemptive change.

The words of Jesus may have been ringing in Paul's ears as he wrote to the Corinthians: "I was hungry and you gave me food, I was thirsty and you gave me something to drink, I was a stranger and you welcomed me" (Matt. 25:35).

Maria Teresa Porcile of Uruguay retells the story of the woman at the well (John 4:1-42) in this way:

> In the shanty-town there was no water . . .
> It was evening, and the day had been very hard. . . .
> And Jesus said: "Give me a drink."
> A woman passed that way, coming from afar. She was a stranger, someone they didn't know and she carried a bucket. She went up to the well where the children were sitting, and the old people and the men and women, looking at the water in the well—the water, so near and yet so far.
> And Jesus said: "Give me a drink."
> And the woman answered: "Why do you ask me for a drink? You are poor and I am rich. You are thirsty but the bucket is mine."
> And Jesus said: "Woman, what of the well? Whose well is it?" And the woman's eyes were opened and with her bucket they began to draw water for the whole district.[2]

Imagine what this new vision of God would mean for us as the church. No more superapostles. Only a community of the Cross, who gives up all power *over* people in order to nurture God's power *for* people and *with* people, a community that *shares* and *fulfills* God's power in this world, a community whose only power is the power of love. Could it be that God wants us to be this kind of community?

Postscript

There were two pieces of feedback that came forth at our next sermon roundtable. Bob felt strongly that his resistance to the idea that God was, in some sense, powerless, had not been represented adequately in the sermon. Because his perspective had been avoided by the group at our meeting, I had treated it with a contrapuntal in the sermon—acknowledging that his perspective existed, but not pursuing it. According to Bob, he had heard feedback after the sermon from others who shared his resistance. He wanted this to be addressed in the next sermon.

Jill and Bert, on the other hand, felt that the sermon had not been practical enough. I apologized, but noted that I had heard the group *begin* to come to terms with the ideas that God gives up power and that God needs us in order to have power, but that our discussion had not gone far enough into the actual implications of these ideas for practice. I did not feel that it was my duty to assert these implications prior to the counsel of the group. The group decided to spend more time in the future trying to determine how to live, in light of the gospel message.

Conclusions

I realize that collaborative preaching will probably take slightly different forms in each congregational context. Demographic and educational differences will generate a variety of emphases in sermon roundtables and in the ways that material from roundtable discussions is used in sermons. As I have already noted, smaller and larger congregations will configure sermon roundtables differently. In some cases, there will be resistance to new procedures and practices. Where collaborative preaching has been tried, it normally takes at least a year for the congregation to "catch on" to how the process works. In larger churches, it may take more time than this. Where it is used consistently, however, and not abandoned in favor of other, more familiar models, the results are often astounding.

The future of communication is clearly in the direction of increased collaboration. Interactive television and computer on-line services suggest many possibilities for broadening collaboration in sermon preparation, as such technology becomes more accessible. Imagine what sermon collaboration might be like if every member of your congregation could contribute each week to an on-line sermon brainstorming meeting!

No matter what form it takes, collaborative preaching can transform the preaching ministry and support an approach to congregational leadership that is more mutual and participative. Over the course of time, collaborative preaching empowers members of a congregation to become interpreters of biblical faith and partners in the mission of the church.

NOTES

PREFACE

1. David J. Hesselgrave, " 'Gold from Egypt': The Contribution of Rhetoric to Cross-Cultural Communication," *Missiology: An International Review* 4 (1976): 95.

2. Nashville: Abingdon Press, 1964, 76-82.

3. Philadelphia: United Church Press, 1972, 75-82.

4. See the cassette tape series by John Killinger entitled "How to Enrich Your Preaching: An Eight-Session Cassette Course for Individual or Group Use" (Nashville: Abingdon Press, Abingdon Audio Graphics, 1975).

5. See Reuel L. Howe, *The Miracle of Dialogue* (New York: The Seabury Press, 1963), and Clyde. H. Reid, "Preaching and the Nature of Communication," *Pastoral Psychology* 14 (1963), 40-49.

6. "Preaching as the Interface of Two Social Worlds: The Congregation as Corporate Agent in the Act of Preaching," Arthur Van Seters, ed., *Preaching as a Social Act: Theology and Practice* (Nashville: Abingdon Press, 1988), 55-93.

7. Minneapolis: Fortress Press, 1993, 21.

1. Preaching and Empowerment

1. See Dean R. Hoge, Benton Johnson, and Donald A. Luidens, *Vanishing Boundaries: The Religion of Mainline Protestant Baby Boomers* (Louisville: Westminster/John Knox Press, 1994).

2. Walter Brueggemann, *The Prophetic Imagination* (Philadelphia: Fortress Press, 1978).

3. William Sloane Coffin, *A Passion for the Possible: A Message to the U. S. Churches* (Louisville: Westminster/John Knox Press, 1993).

4. William H. Willimon, *Peculiar Speech: Preaching to the Baptized* (Grand Rapids: Eerdmans, 1992).

5. J. Randall Nichols, *The Restoring Word: Preaching as Pastoral Communication* (San Francisco: Harper and Row, 1987), 64.

6. See, for instance, Ernesto Cardenal, trans. Donald D. Walsh, *The Gospel in Solentiname*, Vol. I (Maryknoll, N.Y.: Orbis Boks, 1976).

7. For a brief overview of situational studies of leadership, see David W. Johnson and Frank P. Johnson, *Joining Together: Group Theory and Group Skills* (Englewood Cliffs, N.J.: Prentice-Hall, 1991), 156-72.

8. In Regina Coll, C.S.J., "Power, Powerlessness and Empowerment," *Religious Education* 81, no. 3 (Summer 1986): 417.

9. Martha Ellen Stortz, *PastorPower* (Nashville: Abingdon, 1993), 98-121, refers to this as "coactive" power, which is characterized by friendship.

10. Parker Palmer, " 'All the Way Down': A Spirituality of Public Life" in Parker Palmer, Barbara G. Wheeler, and James W. Fowler, eds., *Caring for the Commonweal: Education for Religious and Public Life* (Mercer University Press, 1990), 159.

11. Ibid., 152.

12. Ibid., 152-3.

13. Ibid., 153. According to Palmer, the public realm is not a strictly external, social phenomenon. Palmer parallels the realm of the public with the inner arena of the psychological, with its plurality of selves. Both this inner arena and the outer "public" sphere are "uncharted realms of power where we encounter a strange and alien pluralism."

14. Patrick R. Keifert, *Welcoming the Stranger: A Public Theology of Worship and Evangelism* (Minneapolis: Fortress Press, 1992), 8-9.

15. See Edward Farley, *Good and Evil: Interpreting a Human Condition* (Minneapolis: Augsburg Fortress Press, 1990), 39.

16. Ibid., 41-42.

17. Palmer, "A Spirituality of Public Life," 155.

18. Ibid. Palmer goes on to assert that ". . . inwardly, it takes the form of simple denial that we have a shadow side."

19. Ibid.

20. Ibid.

21. Richard Sennett, *The Fall of Public Man* (New York: Alfred A. Knopf, 1977), 259.

22. *Welcoming the Stranger*, 24.

23. "Private Religion, Individualistic Society, and Common Worship," in Eleanor Bernstein, C.S.J., ed., *Liturgy and Spirituality in Context: Perspectives on Prayer and Culture* (Collegeville, Minn.: The Liturgical Press, 1990), 35.

24. Ibid., 36.

25. Robert Bellah, *Habits of the Heart: Individualism and Commitment in American Life* (Berkeley: University of California Press, 1984), 72, quoted in Bernstein, 34.

26. "A Spirituality of Public Life," 158.

27. *Welcoming the Stranger,* 57.

28. Carl Rahner has pointed out how Christian worship is the redemptive culmination of the "liturgy of the world and its history." "Secular Life and the Sacraments," *The Tablet* (6 March, 1971) 236-38; (13 March, 1971) 267-68. Quoted in Searle, "Private Religion," 41.

29. Ibid., 42-3.

30. Christine Smith, *Preaching as Weeping, Confession and Resistance* (Louisville: Westminster/John Knox Press, 1992).

31. Elaine Ramshaw, *Ritual and Pastoral Care* (Philadelphia: Fortress Press, 1987), 93-95.

32. For more on "leadership at a distance" see Robert Dubin, "Metaphors of Leadership: An Overview," in James G. Hunt and Lars L. Larson, *Crosscurrents in Leadership* (Carbondale and Edwardsville: Southern Illinois University Press, 1979), 225-38.

33. For more on task leadership see Will McWhinney, "The Realities of Leadership," in Robert Tannenbaum, Newton Margulies and Fred Massarik, ed., *Human Systems Development* (San Francisco: Jossey-Bass Publishers, 1987), 294-95.

34. See Mary McKay, "Some Obstacles to Authentic Leadership," in Adrian van Kaam and Susan A. Muto, eds., *Creative Formation of Life and World* (Washington, D.C.: University Press of America, 1982), 439-60. According to McKay, what we are calling alienation and symbiosis "converge in the authoritarian personality." On the one hand, the authoritarian leader is "one whose motivational life is based primarily on satisfaction of deficiencies" and therefore "has an impaired readiness to empathetically perceive other's needs." On the other hand, the authoritarian leader is "one who is incapable of sufficient detachment" and is therefore "liable to have an erroneous perception of those toward whom he or she experiences a spontaneous 'in' movement." McKay, 443.

35. In leadership theory this is sometimes called "follower empowerment." Gilbert W. Fairholm, *Values Leadership: Toward a New Philosophy of Leadership* (New York: Praeger, 1991), 72.

36. See Stanley Hauerwas, "The Pastor as Prophet: Ethical Reflections on an Improbable Mission," in Earl E. Shelp and Ronald Sunderland, eds., *The Pastor as Prophet* (New York: The Pilgrim Press, 1985), 41.

37. Ibid., 40-41.

38. Levinas articulated this notion of "coming to terms" with the other as a fundamental dimension of relationality. See Emmanuel Levinas, *Totality and Infinity,* trans. Alphonso Lingis (Pittsburgh: Duquesne University Press, 1969). See also Steven G. Crowell "Dialogue and Text: Re-marking the Difference," in *The Interpretation of Dialogue,* ed., Tullio Maranhao (Chicago: The University of Chicago Press, 1990), 338-60.

39. My colleague Darrell Guder has heard Professor Stuhlmacher use this phrase in several lectures and speeches.

40. See J. Randall Nichols, *The Restoring Word*, 79. Nichols plays down the usual distinctions between pastoral and prophetic preaching. For Nichols, a fundamental quality of pastoral preaching is that it "loans" a "sense of reality to people." The close relationship between pastoral and prophetic preaching that Nichols exposes parallels the close connection between the "internal" and the "public" realms in Palmer's work.

41. For an excellent study of the persuasive function of Christian theology see David S. Cunningham, *Faithful Persuasion: In Aid of a Rhetoric of Christian Theology* (Notre Dame and London: University of Notre Dame Press, 1991).

42. It is primarily process and feminist theologians who critiqued coercive forms of persuasion. See Charles Hartshorne, "Divine Absoluteness and Divine Relativity" in *Transcendence,* ed. Herbert W. Richardson and Donald R. Cutler, 164-71; John B. Cobb, Jr. and David Ray Griffin, *Process Theology: An Introductory Exposition* (Philadelphia: Westminster Press, 1976), 52-54; and Anna Case-Winters, *God's Power: Traditional Understandings and Contemporary Challenges* (Louisville: Westminster/John Knox Press, 1990).

43. Hans Freiherr von Campenhausen, *Ecclesiastical Authority and Spiritual Power in the Early Church,* trans. J. A. Baker (Stanford: Stanford University Press, 1969), 67-76. Although somewhat overdrawn, it is clear from the picture that von Campenhausen paints that the nature of charisma was dramatically changed by both Jesus and the apostle Paul.

44. See Joseph W. Trigg, "The Charismatic Intellectual: Origen's Understanding of Religious Leadership" in Jerald C. Brauer, Robert M. Grant, and Martin E. Marty, ed., *Church History* (The American Society of Church History, 1981), 7. See Anthony Blasi, *Making Charisma: The Social Construction of Paul's Image* (New Brunswick: Transaction Publishers, 1991) for a rethinking of Paul's charisma as a social construction through which Paul expresses the early church's own self-understandings about religious leadership. See also Martin Hengel, *The Charismatic Leader and His Followers* (New York: The Crossroad Publishing Company, 1981) and John Howard Schutz, *Paul and the Anatomy of Apostolic Authority* (London: Cambridge University Press, 1975).

45. See Michael White, "Social Authority in the House Church Setting and Ephesians 4:1-16," *Restoration Quarterly* 29, no.4 (1987): 209-228.

46. Ibid., 215, 217.

47. Robert Jewett, *Paul: Apostle to America* (Louisville: Westminster/John Knox Press, 1994), 80.

48. Romans 16:15, for instance, refers to five such hosts—Philologus, Julia, Nereus, Nereus's sister, and Olympas—whose names indicate that they were slaves or former slaves.

49. John Koenig, *New Testament Hospitality: Partnership with Strangers as Promise and Mission* (Philadelphia: Fortress Press, 1985), 98.

50. Ibid., 119. Stories such as the sinful woman's anointing of Jesus' feet, the parable of the good Samaritan, the parable of the prodigal son, the stories of Mary and Martha and Zacchaeus and many others demonstrate

the importance of this guest-host theme in Luke's writing. In Acts there appears to be more emphasis on the hosts who become "residential prophets" (2:1-4; 11:27-30; 13:1-3; 15:32-35; 19:1-7; 21:8-9; 21:10).

51. Ibid., 99.

52. Ibid., 109.

53. White, "Social Authority," 221.

54. Ibid., 218.

55. See Romans 16:15. According to Robert Jewett, Philologus and Julia probably represented members of a shared leadership cadre in the early tenement churches. *Paul, Apostle to America,* 80.

2. Toward a Collaborative Homiletic

1. Bernard Swain, *Liberating Leadership: Practical Styles for Pastoral Ministry* (San Francisco: Harper and Row, 1986), 40.

2. Scriptural references to these practices include Numbers 27:21; 1 Sam. 23:9f.; 28:6; Numbers 26:55. For more on this see Arvid S. Kapelrud, "Cult and Prophetic Words," *Studia Theologica* 4 (1950), 5; Yehezkel Kaufmann, *The Religion of Israel* (New York: Schocken Books, 1972), 85, and Sigmund Mowinckel, "Ecstatic Experience and Rational Elaboration in Old Testament Prophecy," *Acta Orientalia* 12 (1935), 272.

3. See Elizabeth A. Castelli, *Imitating Paul: A Discourse of Power* (Louisville: Westminster/John Knox Press, 1991), 56.

4. *Tischreden, Weimarer Ausgabe,* III, 672-74, quoted in T. H. L. Parker, *The Oracles of God: An Introduction to the Preaching of John Calvin* (London: Lutterworth Press, 1947), 46-47.

5. According to Barth "the possibility that God himself speaks when he is spoken of, is not part of the dialectic way as such; it arises rather at the point where this way (speaking of God) comes to an end." Karl Barth, *The Word of God and the Word of Man,* trans. Douglas Horton (New York: Harper and Brothers, 1957), 211.

6. See Helmut Theilicke, *Encounter with Spurgeon* (Grand Rapids: Baker Book House, 1963); James Stewart, *Heralds of God* (Grand Rapids: Baker Book House, 1946); see also Karl Barth, *Homiletics,* trans. Geoffrey W. Bromiley and Donald E. Daniels (Louisville: Westminster/John Knox Press, 1991).

7. Quoted in T. H. L. Parker, *Calvin's Preaching* (Louisville: Westminster/John Knox Press, 1992), 50.

8. Ibid., 53. Calvin understood that "submission to God's message is the work of grace, not nature."

9. Swain, *Liberating Leadership,* 47.

10. Castelli, *Imitating Paul,* 98-101. It could be argued, however, that Paul desired that relationships be grounded in freely given love, rather than in obligatory obedience. Although at times Paul commands *agape* as a by-prod-

uct of relationships of honor and respect (Gal. 5:14; Eph. 5:25), there are far more numerous instances in which he asserts that love is a freely given dimension (fruit) of life lived in the Spirit (Rom. 5:5; 1 Cor. 13; Gal. 5:22; Eph. 3:19; Philem. 4, 8).

11. An enculturated hearer is the presupposition behind several recent approaches to preaching. Using a "cultural-linguistic" model of communication, rather than a sender-message-receiver model, theologians and homileticians are rethinking the way that preaching "informs" the Christian community. See George Lindbeck, *The Nature of Doctrine* (Louisville: Westminster/John Knox Press, 1989) and John S. McClure, *The Four Codes of Preaching: Rhetorical Strategies* (Minneapolis: Fortress Press, 1991).

12. Parker, *Calvin's Preaching*, 39.

13. Ibid., 42. According to Calvin the pulpit is the "throne of God, from which he wills to govern our souls." (1 Tim. 5:20 Sermon XLIII. CO 53.520/40-44).

14. Ibid., 43.

15. Swain, *Liberating Leadership*, 48.

16. Letty Russell, *Growth in Partnership* (Louisville: Westminster/John Knox, 1981), 37.

17. T. W. Adorno coined the word "authoritarian" to describe the type of personality exemplified by Hitler and his chief administrators. *The Authoritarian Personality* (New York: Harper and Brothers, 1950).

18. For one example see Thomas Gordon, "The Challenge of a New Conception of Leadership," *Pastoral Psychology* 51, vol. 6, (Feb. 1955): 15-23.

19. See G. E. Thomas, "Guide to Pastoral Preaching," *Journal of Pastoral Care* 4 (1950), 16.

20. The classic in this area was Edgar Jackson's *How to Preach to People's Needs* (New York: Abingdon Press, 1956). He later developed the arguments of this book further in *A Psychology for Preaching* (Great Neck: Channel Press, Inc., 1961). See also David Belgum, "Preaching and the Stresses of Life," *The Lutheran Quarterly* 20 (1967), 352; Robert Stackel, "Pastoral Preaching," *The Lutheran Quarterly* 20 (1967), 366; and R. M. Pearson "Preaching and the Understanding of the Congregation," *Pastoral Psychology* 10 (1959), 47-46.

21. Lofton Hudson, "Therapeutic Preaching," *Review and Expositor* 49 (1965), 295.

22. See Russell Dicks, *Pastoral Work and Personal Counseling* (New York: Macmillan, 1944).

23. Harry Levinson, "The Trouble with Sermons," *The Journal of Pastoral Care* 22 (1968), 66-67.

24. M. Furgeson, "Preaching and the Personality of the Preacher," *Pastoral Psychology* 10 (1959), 9-14.

25. See Dan O. Via, *The Parables: Their Literary and Existential Dimension* (Philadelphia: Fortress Press, 1967) and Amos Wilder, *The Language of the Gospel* (Cambridge: Harvard University Press, 1970).

26. See especially Reuel L. Howe, *The Miracle of Dialogue* (Greenwich, Conn.: The Seabury Press, 1963); "Overcoming the Barriers to Communication," *Pastoral Psychology* 14 (1963), 26-32; "Rediscovery of Dialogue in Preaching," *Pastoral Psychology* 12 (1961), 10-14; G. W. Jones, "Proclamation Is Dialogue—Not Monologue," *Theology Today* 24 (1968), 509-511; H. B. Adams, "Revelation in Light of Communication Theory," *Encounter* 25 (1964), 470-475; D. S. Hobbs, "Give and Take on Psychology and Preaching," *Pastoral Psychology* 15 (1964), 53-59; C. H. Reid, "Preaching and the Nature of Communication," *Pastoral Psychology* 14 (1963), 40-49; "Toward a Theology of Communication," *Religious Education* 69 (1974), 355-364.

27. Fred Craddock, *As One Without Authority* (Nashville: Abingdon Press, 1971), 29.

28. Ibid.

29. Ibid., 57.

30. Ibid.

31. Ibid., 64.

32. Ibid., 91.

33. Eugene Lowry, *The Homiletical Plot* (Atlanta: John Knox Press, 1980). According to Lowry, the "stages of the homiletical plot" are (1) Upsetting the Equilibrium, (2) Analyzing the Discrepancy, (3) Disclosing the Clue to Resolution, (4) Experiencing the Gospel, and (5) Anticipating the Consequences.

34. Jackson Carroll, *As One With Authority* (Louisville: Westminster/John Knox Press, 1991), 73.

35. See Robin Meyers, *With Ears to Hear: Preaching as Self-Persuasion* (Cleveland, Ohio: The Pilgrim Press, 1993). Meyers's aproach to preaching is similar to Craddock's. According to Meyers, "a highly developed empathetic imagination" is essential to preaching in which the listener is "the dominant partner in the persuasion process" (29). See also Craig A. Loscalzo, *Preaching Sermons that Connect: Effective Communication Through Identification* (Downer's Grove, Ill.: InterVarsity Press, 1992).

36. Swain, *Liberating Leadership*, 81.

37. Ibid., 82. According to Swain, interchangeability means that "no one person . . . can perform very much of his or her leadership effectively without others' help."

38. Hans-Georg Gadamer, *Truth and Method,* trans. Garrett Barden and John Cumming (New York: Seabury Press, 1975), 273, 337. Steven Crowell observes that for Gadamer, "dialogue is said to consist in the symmetrical movement toward a fusion of horizons between reciprocally self-effacing participants who 'risk' inherited prejudices within a common interrogative orientation toward the truth . . ." Steven Crowell, "Dialogue and Text: Re-marking the Difference" in Tullio Maranhao, ed., *The Interpretation of Dialogue* (Chicago: University of Chicago Press, 1990), 347.

39. Crowell, "Dialogue," 354.

40. See the nine-dot puzzle on page 52 of *The Homiletical Plot.*

41. There is little difference between the logic of Craddock's "inductive trip" and Lowry's "upset equilibrium" and "clues to resolution."

42. See *S/Z*, trans. Richard Miller (New York: Hill and Wang, 1974).

43. *The Homiletical Plot*, 48.

44. See *With Ears to Hear*, 84-87.

45. Will McWhinney makes this distinction to describe forms of participation in which there is only a "shared perception of imposed policy." "The Realities of Leadership" in Robert Tannenbaum, Newton Margulies, Fred Massarik and Associates eds., *Human Systems Development* (San Francisco: Jossey-Bass Publishers, 1987), 294.

46. To some extent, the sense of being manipulated that sometimes accompanies inductive and narrative preaching is a product of the canons of narrative and inductive logic themselves. The reality of participation is lost because the preacher is relying first on a standard form of argumentation (induction) and second on standard literary tropes and devises of anticipatory plot (narration).

3. Collaborative Preaching

1. The back and forth movement of dialogue is the soil in which collaboration grows. We know a great deal more about the language and practice of dialogue than we knew in the 1960s, when the dialogue preaching movement began. It is now time to return to dialogue and ask if what we have learned adds anything that might yield a form of preaching that would be more dialogical than either inductive or narrative preaching. I have chosen to use the word *conversation* instead of *dialogue* to describe such preaching in order to move the discussion of dialogue from the level of an ideal to the level of practice. Conversation is the linguistic stuff of dialogue. Dialogue is an ideal that conversation only approximates as it takes certain forms.

2. Conversation analysis is an outgrowth of the field of *discourse analysis*. Whereas discourse analysis is concerned with identifying the symbolic and idiomatic aspects of language use in a specific context (thematics and style), conversation analysis "studies the organization of everyday talk, of language as actually used in social interaction." Michael Moerman, *Talking Culture: Ethnography and Conversation Analysis* (Philadelphia: University of Pennsylvania Press, 1988), x.

3. Ibid., xi.

4. Dennis K. Mumby calls this kind of conversation "radical conversation," because it includes an ongoing critique of the "sociopolitical milieu" in which it is embedded. *Communication and Power in Organizations: Discourse, Ideology, and Domination* (Norwood, N.J.: Ablex Publishing Corp., 1988), 133.

5. Chuck Lathrop, "In Search of a Roundtable," in *A Gentle Presence.* Washington, D.C.: Appalachian Documentation (ADOC), 1977, 7.

6. See Paul Drew, "Asymmetries of Knowledge in Conversational Interactions," in Ivana Markova and Klaus Foppa, eds. *Asymmetries in Dialogue* (Savage, Md.: Barnes and Noble Books, 1991), 21-47.

7. Gadamer argued against dialectics on this precise point. According to Gadamer, the " 'experience of dialogue' " is " 'not limited to the sphere of giving reasons and counterreasons, in whose exchange and unification the meaning of every conflict can find its end.' Rather there is 'still something else' found in such experience, 'a potentiality for being-other which lies over and beyond any coming to terms by way of what is in common.' " Quoted from *Verständiguing in Gemeinsamen* in Crowell, "Dialogue and Text, Re-marking the Difference," in Tullio Maranhao, ed., *The Interpretation of Dialogue* (Chicago: University of Chicago Press, 1990), 350.

8. See Sharon Welch, *A Feminist Ethic of Risk* (Minneapolis: Fortress Press, 1989), 127. Welsh criticizes liberal ethicists who posit what Seyla Benhabib calls the "generalized other," as the partner in moral dialogue. Quoting Benhabib, Welsh asserts that when each individual is seen as " 'a rational being entitled to the same rights and duties we would want to ascribe to ourselves,' " there "is no need to take into account 'the individuality and concrete identity of the other.' "

9. Ibid., 126.

10. See Johanna Bos, "Solidarity with the Stranger," in *A Journey to Justice,* a collection of essays published by the Presbyterian Committee on the Self-Development of People, 1993. In this paper, Professor Bos argues for the use of the term *solidarity* to capture the meaning of the biblical concept of hospitality.

11. See also Thomas W. Ogletree, *Hospitality to the Stranger: Dimensions of Moral Understanding* (Philadelphia: Fortress Press, 1945).

12. Crowell, "Dialogue and Text," 355. According to Crowell, "Dialogue is neither a fusion of horizons (Gadamer) nor a site of endless deferrals (Derrida), but the creation of commonplaces governed by justice, or the giving-welcoming of the Other as stranger . . . (Levinas)." (parentheses mine)

13. See ibid., 354.

14. The use of the word *reality* here is meant to imply what Sharon Welch calls a "material basis" for communication which she locates in solidarity. It is not enough simply to extend conversations to include the voices of women and other heretofore marginalized voices, assuming that some "universal and unconstrained consensus" can be reached between all parties. More important is to allow a substantive "mutual critique" to exist in which the concrete, substantive proposals of each party contribute to the promise of "a universal solidarity of human beings." Welch, *A Feminist Ethic of Risk,* 132.

15. See William A. Beardslee, John B. Cobb, Jr., David J. Lull, Russell Pageant, Theodore J. Weeden, Sr., Barry A. Woodbridge, *Biblical Preaching on the Death of Jesus* (Nashville: Abingdon Press, 1989), 41.

16. " 'Gold from Egypt': The Contribution of Rhetoric to Cross-Cultural Communication," *Missiology: An International Review* 4 (1976): 95.

4. Collaborative Brainstorming: A Word to Preachers

1. The suggestion to call these groups sermon roundtables, instead of sermon preparation roundtables, was made by Al Krumenacher at a meeting of the Homiletical Feast in Dallas, Texas in January, 1994.

2. See Jackson Carroll, *As One With Authority* (Louisville: Westminster/John Knox, 1991), 100. According to Carroll, interpretation of meaning "is aimed at assisting the congregation and its members to reflect on and interpret their life, individually and corporately, in light of God's purposes in Jesus Christ . . . to break open the symbols of the tradition in such a way that they illumine the concrete and sometimes threatening issues of life, personal and social, in fresh and helpful ways."

5. The Language of Collaboration: What It Sounds Like

1. Some leadership theorists call the topic-setting role of leaders "values leadership." See Gilbert W. Fairholm, *Values Leadership: Toward a New Philosophy of Leadership* (New York: Praeger Press, 1991), 65. According to Fairholm, leaders "serve as values clarifiers and as communicators of values throughout the organization."

2. Quoted from Ioanna Dimitracopoulou, *Conversational Competence and Social Development* (Cambridge: Cambridge University Press, 1990), 19.

3. The summons is the most homiletically useful of a set of "role-taking" exercises that occur in informal conversations. By means of these exercises roles are distributed in a conversation along topical lines. Other role-taking exercises are greetings, enquiries into personal states, and topic elicitors. See Graham Button and John R. E. Lee, *Talk and Social Organization* (Philadelphia: Multilingual Matters, 1987), 35, 38.

4. Angela Keppler and Thomas Luckmann, " 'Teaching': Conversational Transmission of Knowledge" in Ivana Markova and Klaus Foppa eds., *Asymmetries in Dialogue* (Savage, Md.: Barnes and Noble Books, 1991), 145. According to Keppler and Luckmann, "This does not mean that conversation yields to another genre of communication. . . . Conversational teaching remains an enclave within conversation."

5. *Homiletic: Moves and Structures* (Philadelphia: Fortress Press, 1987), 47.

6. "Following" is a dynamic attributed to topics (subjects) and topic-setting. "Linkage" has to do with the setting of predicates, not subjects for discussion.

7. See Gail Jefferson, "On Exposed and Embedded Correction in Conversation," in Graham Button and John R. E. Lee, ed., *Talk and Social Organization* (Philadelphia: Multilingual Matters, 1987), 86-93.

8. *That's Not What I Meant!: How Conversational Style Makes or Breaks Relationships* (New York: Ballentine Books, 1987), 74.

9. Ibid., 91. According to Tannen, "The framing that is going on at any moment is part of what establishes the frame for what goes on next, and is partly created by the framing that went before. The footing we establish at any momemt is occasioned by the footing that was established the moment before—and the year before."

10. See ibid., 86.

11. Ibid., 87.

12. *The Restoring Word: Preaching as Pastoral Communication* (San Francisco: Harper and Row, 1987), 69. Nichols associates re-framing with "prophesying." According to Nichols, "what the prophet does is not so much forecast the future as take a look at things-as-they-are and point out different connections and meanings from what most people are seeing . . ."

13. See Robert E. Sanders, *Cognitive Foundations of Calculated Speech: Controlling Understandings in Conversation and Persuasion* (Albany: SUNY Press, 1987), 207-228.

14. Andrew King asserts that the "postmodern obsession with narrative" is due to the fact that "it arises from local practice." The articulation of objective arguments by a privileged elite has given way in our day and age to the narrating of the specific, unique, often alien stories of those on the periphery. "What Is Postmodern Rhetoric?" in Andrew King, ed., *Postmodern Political Communication: The Fringe Challenges the Center* (Westport, Conn.: Praeger Publishers, 1992), 6.

15. From a sermon on II Corinthians 4:13–5:1 preached by Marian McClure on May 5, 1994 at James Lees Memorial Presbyterian Church, Louisville, Kentucky. This story is paraphrased from a sermon by Susan Hagood Lee "Witness To Christ, Witness to Pain; One Woman's Journey Through Wife Battering," in Annie Lally Milhaven, ed. *Sermons Seldom Heard: Women Proclaim Their Lives* (New York: Crossroad, 1991), 14-15.

6. A Case Study

1. Grace D. Cumming Long, *Passion and Reason: Womenviews of Christian Life* (Louisville: Westminster/John Knox Press, 1993), 47.

2. Maria Theresa Porcile of Uruguay, "Water in the Slums," in *New Eyes for Reading: Biblical and Theological Reflections by Women from the Third World*, ed. John S. Pobee and Bärbel von Wartenberg-Potter (Geneva: WCC, 1986), 28. Used by permission.

B I B L I O G R A P H Y

Homiletics

Barr, Browne. *Parish Back Talk.* Nashville: Abingdon Press, 1964.

Barr, Browne and Mary Eakin. *The Ministering Congregation.* Philadelphia: United Church Press, 1972.

Buttrick, David. *Homiletic: Moves and Structures.* Minneapolis: Fortress Press, 1987.

Cardenal, Ernesto. *The Gospel in Solentiname, Vol. I,* trans. Donald D. Walsh. Maryknoll, N. Y.: Orbis Books, 1976.

Coffin, William Sloane. *A Passion for the Possible: A Message to the U. S. Churches.* Louisville: Westminster/John Knox Press, 1993.

Craddock, Fred. *As One Without Authority.* Nashville: Abingdon Press, 1971.

Loscalzo, Craig A. *Preaching Sermons that Connect: Effective Communication Through Identification.* Downer's Grove, Ill.: Intervarsity Press, 1992.

Lowry, Eugene. *The Homiletical Plot.* Atlanta: John Knox Press, 1980.

McClure, John S. *The Four Codes of Preaching: Rhetorical Strategies.* Minneapolis: Fortress Press, 1991.

Meyers, Robin. *With Ears to Hear: Preaching as Self-Persuasion.* Cleveland, Ohio: The Pilgrim Press, 1993.

Moeller, Pamela Ann. *Kinesthetic Homiletic: Embodying Gospel in Preaching.* Minneapolis: Fortress Press, 1993.

Nichols, J. Randall. *The Restoring Word: Preaching as Pastoral Communication.* San Francisco: Harper and Row, 1987.

Smith, Christine. *Preaching as Weeping, Confession and Resistance.* Louisville: Westminster/John Knox Press, 1992.

Wardlaw, Don. "Preaching as the Interface of Two Social Worlds: The Congregation as Corporate Agent in the Act of Preaching." In *Preaching as a Social Act: Theology and Practice,* ed., Arthur Van Seters (Nashville: Abingdon Press, 1988), 55-93.

Leadership

Adorno, T. W. *The Authoritarian Personality.* New York: Harper and Brothers, 1950.

Burns, James MacGregor, *Leadership.* New York: Harper and Row, 1978.

Bradley, Raymond Trevor. *Charisma and Social Structure: A Study of Love, Power, Wholeness and Transformation.* New York: Paragon House, 1987.

Carothers, J. Edward. *The Paralysis of Mainstream Protestant Leadership.* Nashville: Abingdon Press, 1990.

Carroll, Jackson. *As One With Authority.* Louisville: Westminster/John Knox Press, 1991.

Fairholm, Gilbert W. *Values Leadership: Toward a New Philosophy of Leadership.* New York: Praeger, 1991.

Falbo, Toni, B. Lynn New, and Margie Gaines. "Perceptions of Authority and the Power Strategies Used by Clergymen," *Journal for the Scientific Study of Religion* 26 (Dec., 1987): 499-507.

Gilman, Andrew. "Ordination Tasks: Five Clusters," *Quarterly Review* 1 (Spr. 1982): 87-95.

Graumann, Carl F., and Serge Moscovici, eds. *Changing Conceptions of Leadership.* New York: Springer-Verlag, 1986.

Hunt, James G., and Lars L. Larson, ed. *Crosscurrents in Leadership.* Carbondale: Southern Illinois University Press, 1979.

Hutch, Richard A. "Types of Women Religious Leaders," *Religion* 14 (1984): 155-73.

Johnson, David W., and Frank P. Johnson. *Joining Together: Group Theory and Group Skills.* Englewood Cliffs, N.J.: Prentice-Hall, 1991.

Kaam, Adrian van and Susan A. Muto, ed. *Creative Formation of Life and World.* Washington, D. C.: University Press of America, 1982.

Kellerman, Barbara, ed. *Leadership: Multidisciplinary Perspectives.* Englewood Cliffs, N. J. Prentice-Hall, 1984.

Rausch, Thomas P. *Authority and Leadership in the Church: Past Directions and Future Possibilities.* Wilmington, Del.: Michael Glazier, 1989.

Rosenbach, William E., and Robert L. Taylor. *Contemporary Issues in Leadership.* Boulder: Westview Press, 1984.

Russell, Letty. *Growth in Partnership.* Louisville: Westminster/John Knox Press, 1981.

Schaller, Lyle E. *Strategies for Change.* Nashville: Abingdon Press, 1993.

Schein, Edgar H. *Organizational Culture and Leadership.* San Francisco: Jossey-Bass Publishers, 1992.

Steele, David A. *Images of Leadership and Authority for the Church: Biblical Principles and Secular Models.* Lanham: University Press of America, 1986.

Stortz, Martha Ellen. *PastorPower.* Nashville: Abingdon Press, 1993.

Swain, Bernard, *Liberating Leadership: Practical Styles for Pastoral Ministry.* San Francisco: Harper and Row, 1986.

Tannenbaum, Robert, Newton Margulies, and Fred Massarik, eds. *Human Systems Development.* San Francisco: Jossey-Bass Publishers, 1987.

Conversation

Bublitz, Wolfram. *Supportive Fellow-Speakers and Cooperative Conversations.* Amsterdam/Philadelphia: John Benjamins Publishing Co., 1988.

Button, Graham, and John R. E. Lee. *Talk and Social Organization.* Philadelphia: Multilingual Matters, 1987.

Dimitracopoulou, Ioanna. *Conversational Competence and Social Development.* Cambridge University Press, 1990.

Gadamer, Hans-Georg. *Truth and Method,* trans. Garrett Barden and John Cumming. New York: Seabury Press, 1975.

Hovland, Carl I., Irving L. Janis, and Harold H. Kelley, *Communication and Persuasion: Psychological Studies of Opinion Change.* Westport, Conn.: Greenwood Press, 1982.

Howe, Reuel L. *The Miracle of Dialogue.* New York: The Seabury Press, 1963.

King, Andrew, ed. *Postmodern Political Communication: The Fringe Challenges the Center.* Westport, Conn.: Praeger Publishers, 1992.

Levinas, Emmanuel. *Totality and Infinity,* trans. Alphonso Lingis. Pittsburgh: Duquesne University Press, 1969.

Maranhao, Tullio, ed. *The Interpretation of Dialogue.* University of Chicago Press, 1990.

Markova, Ivana, and Klaus Foppa, eds. *Asymmetries in Dialogue.* Savage, Md.: Barnes and Noble Books, 1991.

Moerman, Michael. *Talking Culture: Ethnology and Conversation Analysis.* Philadelphia: University of Pennsylvania Press, 1988.

Mumby, Dennis K. *Communication and Power in Organizations: Discourse, Ideology, and Domination.* Norwood, N.J.: Ablex Publishing Corp., 1988.

Placher, William C. *Unapologetic Theology: A Christian Voice in a Pluralistic Conversation.* Louisville: Westminster/John Knox Press, 1989.

Sanders, Robert E. *Cognitive Foundations of Calculated Speech: Controlling Understandings in Conversation and Persuasion.* Albany: SUNY Press, 1987.

Tannen, Deborah. *That's Not What I Meant! How Conversational Style Makes or Breaks Relationships.* New York: Ballentine Books, 1987.

Welch, Sharon. *A Feminist Ethic of Risk.* Minneapolis: Fortress Press, 1989.

Biblical and Theological Resources

Blausi, Anthony. *Making Charisma: The Social Construction of Paul's Image.* New Brunswick: Transaction Publishers, 1991.

Case-Winters, Anna. *God's Power: Traditional Understandings and Contemporary Challenges.* Louisville: Westminster/John Knox Press, 1990.

Castelli, Elizabeth A. *Imitating Paul: A Discourse of Power.* Louisville: Westminster/John Knox Press, 1991.

Campenhausen, Hans Freiherr von. *Ecclesiastical Authority and Spiritual Power in the Early Church,* trans. J. A. Baker. Stanford University Press, 1969.

Cunningham, David S. *Faithful Persuasion: In Aid of a Rhetoric of Christian Theology.* University of Notre Dame Press, 1991.

Farley, Edward. *Good and Evil: Interpreting a Human Condition.* Minneapolis: Augsburg Fortress Press, 1990.

Hengel, Martin. *The Charismatic Leader and His Followers.* New York: The Crossroad Publishing Company, 1981.

Jewett, Robert. *Paul: Apostle to America.* Louisville: Westminster/John Knox Press, 1994.

Keifert, Patrick R. *Welcoming the Stranger: A Public Theology of Worship and Evangelism.* Minneapolis: Fortress Press, 1992.

Koenig, John. *New Testament Hospitality: Partnership with Strangers as Promise and Mission.* Philadelphia: Fortress Press, 1985.

Ogletree, Thomas W. *Hospitality to the Stranger: Dimensions of Moral Understanding.* Philadelphia: Fortress Press, 1945.

Palmer, Parker. *The Company of Strangers: Christians and the Renewal of America's Public Life.* New York: Crossroad Publishing Company, 1981.

Palmer, Parker, Barbara G. Wheeler, James W. Fowler, eds. *Caring for the Commonweal: Education for Religious and Public Life.* Macon, Ga.: Mercer University Press, 1990.

Schutz, John Howard. *Paul and the Anatomy of Apostolic Authority.* London: Cambridge University Press, 1975.

White, Michael. "Social Authority in the House Church Setting and Ephesians 4:1-16," *Restoration Quarterly* 29, no. 4, (1987): 209-28.

INDEX

INDEX